Mary W. M[...]
55 Walcott
Jamestown

For Ed Connelly with
sincere best wishes. —

[signature]
Aug 29, 1992

STARS AND SWASTIKAS

—————————— The Boy Who
Wore Two Uniforms

STARS AND SWASTIKAS

The Boy Who
Wore Two Uniforms

WALTER K. SCHRODER

Archon Books

1992

The paper used in this publication meets minimum requirements
of American National Standard for Information Science-Permanence
of Paper for Printed Library Materials, ANSI Z39.48—1948. ⊗

Library of Congress Cataloging-in-Publication Data

Schröder, Walter, 1928–
Stars and swastikas : the boy who wore
two uniforms / Walter Schröder.
p.   cm.
Includes bibliographical references (p. 189).
1. Schröder, Walter, 1928– .
2. World War, 1939–1945—Personal narratives, American.
3. World War, 1939–1945—Germany.
4. Germany—History—1933–1945. 5. National socialism.
6. German Americans—Biography. I. Title.
D811.S334 1992   940.54′8173—dc20   92-5564
ISBN 0-208-02322-4 (alk. paper)

Dedicated to the God that watched over us;
to my comrades in grey and khaki; to all those who cared;
and to my father who did what he thought was right.

To my daughter Leah:
May your generation bear the fruits of our changing world.

To everything there is a season,
    and a time to every purpose under the heaven:
A time to be born, and a time to die;
    a time to plant, and a time to pluck up
    that which is planted;
A time to kill, and a time to heal;
    a time to break down, and a time to build up;
A time to weep, and a time to laugh;
    a time to mourn, and a time to dance;
A time to cast away stones,
    and a time to gather stones together;
    a time to embrace,
    and a time to refrain from embracing;
A time to get, and a time to lose;
    a time to keep, and a time to cast away;
A time to rend, and a time to sew;
    a time to keep silence, and a time to speak;
A time to love, and a time to hate;
    a time of war, and a time of peace.

ECCLESIASTES 3:1–9

Contents

Preface

The idea of sharing my experiences with others was conceived many years ago, soon after I returned to America in 1952. I had spent most of my youth in Germany and Europe caught up in international hostility, often playing an active and even controversial role that was dictated by circumstance more than by personal choice.

Though I was born in America, going "home" to Germany as a minor in the company of my German parents was certainly not unusual. I had grown up in New York in German surroundings, so Germany, across the Atlantic, was an extension of my normal environment. I was German; joining the Hitler Youth and being drafted during the war, even at the early age of fifteen, were the dictates of the times. No one had to knock on doors to demand that I go. I went with the rest of the kids; it was our duty and we were ready. War and propaganda breed bitterness. How could I like the Americans—even though they came from my birthplace—when they were bombing our homes and cities?

But when the war was over, I faced a rude awakening. The things I had been indoctrinated to believe in were shattered. The uniforms, the pomp, the glitter, all had been facades. Once they were torn down, the real ugliness and bare hatred against classes of fellow humans were revealed. Horror and brutality remain after glory and dreams have faded. Everyone was made to feel the shame, the guilty as well as the innocent. Being German in the eyes of the world was a disgrace. As a family, we faced our own misery, torn apart and separated by the barbed wire and mine-fields the Soviets laid down right through the heart of Germany, isolating my family's home behind the Iron Curtain and leaving me alone on the other side, among the free. But when told I was an American and could become a GI right there in Germany, I knew fate was with me and that things could be made right.

Until now, it never seemed the time to tell my story, to set the record straight, to acknowledge the many people, "enemy" per-sonnel as well as friends, who helped me and my family. At first I kept quiet because of the understandable suspicion of all things German after the war. Then, in the McCarthy era, there was the need to stay clear of contacts with friends in the Communist empire. Finally, there was the possibility of endangering the poor people "on the other side," just by trying to get in touch. In turn, these influences kept me from wanting to publish these memoirs. Times have changed, however, and these obstacles are no longer a factor.

I have pored over my notes, begun in 1952; I have done extensive historical research over the years; and I have located many people the world over, even total strangers, who shared in my experiences. And although the research process can continue infinitely (there is always one more book to read, one more source to track down), it has progressed as far as reasonably possible. The real inspiration to proceed, however, came to me in the sanctuary of my church one day, and I knew then that I should finally share the thoughts that have been buried in the depths of my mind for a good part of my life.

For helping me get the project off the ground, I first and foremost wish to thank Dr. John A. Roche III, a good neighbor and professor at Rhode Island College, for his interest from the very beginning. He was one of the first people in whom I confided and with whom I shared my thoughts and ideas. I also thank him for his unabated patience and for so generously giving of his time, first listening and counseling, and then reviewing and correcting drafts of the many episodes and experiences I tried to relay over a period of time.

For his encouragement and straightforward appraisals of my

story and its appeal to the public, I thank Peter Crolius, of Wickford, a professional in the book business and himself a well established writer.

I wish to extend a particularly special word of appreciation to the editor of *Pegasus*, the journal of the British Parachute Regiment, for assisting me in establishing contact with members of the 6th Airborne Armoured Reconnaissance Regiment who ran up against my German flak unit in April 1945. As a result of his efforts I am delighted to now list Jack Banbery, Tom Buckley, Gerry James and Owen Kendall—all British paratroopers who faced me in combat just a few yards away—among my new-found friends. I thank each of them for describing to me our battlefield encounter as observed from their respective vantage points.

I acknowledge Gilbert Debecker, author, and Rene Janssens, both of Belgium, for being extremely supportive in helping me reconstruct my days as a POW at Camp 2228, with photographs and written materials which they so graciously supplied.

Special thanks to Chuck Simons for sharing his collection of World War II unit histories, allowing me to pinpoint the American units that occupied my former hometown in Germany while I was away as a POW of the British. In addition, I thank the Associations of the 76th Infantry Division and the 354 Infantry Regiment for supplying me with copies of their unit histories; and also Alfred H. Pepin, Jr., a former member of the 353d Infantry, for sharing his personal experiences from the days his unit occupied areas near my former residence in Germany.

Special thanks to Dr. Hans-Dietrich Nicolaisen, of Germany, himself a former antiaircraft auxiliarist and postwar author, for scanning his personal research files and supplying me with information on my World War II flak unit; and to my former schoolmate and Luftwaffenhelfer comrade, Eberhard Leithold from East Germany, for spotting wartime pictures of me in his photo album and sending them to me after being out of touch for forty-five years. I extend my appreciation also to Erich Siegel and Hans W. Nussmann, both of Germany, who as POWs experienced, as I did, the deprivations of Camp 2228.

And lest I forget, my heartfelt thanks go to my dear mother, a subject of this book, for recalling at my urging more than once her experiences in Germany, first under American and later, Soviet occupation. Also, to Alfred Schroeder, my photographer friend, and member of the Council on America's Military Past, my sincere appreciation for his photographic support during the research phase of this undertaking.

A number of U.S. governmental offices and institutions were extremely cooperative in providing photographs and archival materials having a direct bearing on the project. I appreciate their help and I thank each of them. They include: the National Archives, Washington; the National Aeronautical and Space Museum; and the Department of the Air Force Audio Visual Detachment.

For their assistance in the earlier phases of my research, I thank the Ministry of Defence, Whitehall, England; the Imperial War Museum for locating subject related photography; and the University of Keele for furnishing aerial photography of my German flak unit taken by a U.S. reconnaissance plane on my birthday in 1945, just four days before we were overrun by British paratroops.

A special word of appreciation to the Deutsche Dienststelle (WASt) in Berlin, for providing me with basic personnel data enabling me to trace wartime acquaintances in Germany. I am also indebted to the Bibliothek fuer Zeitgeschichte in Stuttgart and the Institut fuer Zeitgeschichte in Munich for their help in acquiring information on certain military personalities and also in searching out photos supporting the manuscript text; to the city archives of Frankfurt for photographic support; and to the city of Minden, Westfalia for making available wartime bombing and casualty data. Also, many thanks to the Bayerisches Hauptstaatsarchiv, Munich, for information on the retrieval of Hitler documents during my tour of duty in Munich.

Last, but not least, I must note that without the staunch support of my own family, my wife Lora and daughter Leah, my project would still be on hold. Their interest, understanding, tolerance and encouragement were essential to the completion of this work. For this, I am eternally grateful.

Achtung!

I am Luftwaffenhelfer (LWH) Walter Schröder of the 4./434 Schwere Flak Abteilung, a heavy antiaircraft battery of twelve 88mm guns emplaced in the fields west of the town of Stemmer and within 300 meters of Holzhausen II/Brede. We are situated next to the country road to Minden-on-Weser in Westfalia, northwest Germany. The Mittelland Kanal, with its aqueduct over the Weser River at Minden, a town about six kilometers down the road in a southeasterly direction, is just to the south of our positions.

The Wiehen Mountain range, which runs east-west, forms our horizon ten kilometers to the south. The navigable canal runs in the same direction to the north of the mountain range. Another battery of 88s manned by Italians is emplaced 150 meters to the east of our site. Operating with a joint Command Post, we are a *Gross Batterie*, with the firepower of twenty heavy 88s. We are tasked with protecting the aqueduct against air attack and laying down, in coordination with several other batteries in the Minden area, a barrier of antiaircraft fire to destroy enemy aircraft enroute to targets farther east.

Planes of the U.S. Eighth Air Force inflicted damage to the canal during raids on 26 October and 6 December 1944, despite the barrage of fire and shrapnel from our 88s. During such engagements we keep firing in front of the lead plane, forcing the others to fly smack into the hell of hot exploding steel. We were credited with downing one or more of the "terror bombers" around that time and were awarded permission to add another stripe to our gun tubes and range finder as a sign of another kill. So far, we have seven to our credit with a few more in the process of being verified. That's pretty good, but we have to do much better if we are to stop them. Right now the large bomber formations attacking our cities daily manage to tie up some 900,000 of our men and 10,000 artillery pieces that are sorely needed to stop or slow down the Russians.

Of late, the Flying Fortress and Liberator formations are escorted by fighters; that puts even more enemy planes into the skies above us. On a clear day the contrails give away the approaching bombers while they are still at great distances. We can readily spot these oncoming formations, often with hundreds of planes each, and we keep a watchful eye on them as they draw closer, into our range of fire.

They know we are directly in their flight path, waiting for them to get close enough so we can let go with our 88s and send thousands of pieces of ragged steel their way. Once our battery commander gives the *Feuer Frei* command, they're sitting ducks at the mercy of fate. Our gun crews are trained to fire twenty rounds per minute and will keep firing as long as the planes are coming at us and the firing bell keeps ringing. The enemy pilots and bombardiers have nowhere to go but through it—all the way— or go down. They must be very tense during the approach and even more so during the overflight through the barrage of fire.

We hold our breath while the roar of their engines thunders overhead, and we nervously await the whistling sound of falling bombs among the bursts and explosions of our shells high in the sky. There is always the fear that the bombers may annihilate us by laying down a *Bombenteppich*, a bomb carpet, over the entire length and width of our positions, as has been done elsewhere.

Once a formation is out of range, another battery farther east will take over and open fire to shower them with a new barrage of shrapnel.

Most of our gun crews and the personnel of the range finder section are fifteen- and sixteen-year-old high school students who have been drafted in a group to serve as auxiliarists with this flak unit of the Luftwaffe under the "Total War" concept which integrates the Hitler Youth in the overall defense effort.

After being inducted in January 1944 and following a period of indoctrination as a plotting board operator, several of us were assigned to the range finder crew. Ever since transferring as a unit from the Dessau area to Stemmer, late in the fall of 1944, we have been busy digging in. Now, on 4 April 1945, we are finally finished. The gun crews just yesterday completed the trenches on the west side of their assigned area, while we at the range finder site dug individual foxholes and scattered grass seed around the parapets surrounding the Command Post and our squad huts right next to the command center. The CP serving the combined German and Italian batteries consists of a radar, two range finders and a joint communications facility, clustered 100 meters to the north of the emplaced 88s of the two batteries.

Now we are wondering if we will ever see the grass grow, what with the fast breaking news of the rapid advances of the Allies approaching from the west. We have been on around-the-clock alert ever since word was received yesterday of heavy fighting in the Ibbenbueren-Osnabrueck area some fifty–sixty kilometers west of here. It was a sleepless night for us, with nothing more than a catnap here and there, fully dressed, ready for action at any moment. According to early morning reports, the Allies are pushing forward in force on all highways and secondary roads to the north and south of the Wiehen Mountains. This could very well be the day for our baptism of fire in ground combat; who knows?

We're about as ready as can be under the circumstances. The boys know their business in the operation of their assigned crew-served weapons, but there has not been time to drill for ground combat. A few rifles have been distributed within the last few days, but these are of foreign origin and appear antiquated, perhaps from an earlier campaign. A single antitank gun has been assigned to our battery and emplaced in the open field just north of the CP. This poor location is behind the gun battery as viewed from the road. Therefore the field of fire of this brand new artillery piece is obstructed by the emplacements of the 88s. It really doesn't matter much; we don't have a crew trained to serve this tank-destroying weapon anyway. Besides, it stands there in the open, unprotected, a perfect target for any trained tank gunner.

When we assembled at dawn this morning, we all had a funny feeling about the coming day. We decided to put on our best clothes, our Sunday uniforms, new socks and the best shoes or boots we could muster, just in case. Someone watching might think we were getting ready to go on leave or preparing to make the supreme sacrifice. In fact, we just want to be sure we're ready to move out at a moment's notice, and also that we will survive should all go wrong. Once we leave the positions for whatever reason, it is doubtful that we will be able to return should we forget something. So, satchels and knapsacks are packed and stashed in our dugout next to the range finder.

As we are standing around in the early morning chill just as the sun is about to rise, I wonder if this will be our final day at Stemmer. As long as our guns keep the enemy at bay, we should be alright, but I hesitate to think what might happen if we come up against enemy infantry. We just don't have the weapons to defend ourselves. Only a few of us were issued the old rifles, but all of us did receive a brief indoctrination in the use of the Panzerfaust, a hand held antitank weapon. What good will a Panzerfaust be if we are attacked by troops on foot? Oberleutnant Schrader, our battery commander, has announced that units of the 5th U.S. Armored Division are moving toward Minden on the far side of the Wiehen Mountains. It's just about 9:00 a.m. and it seems certain that we will encounter the enemy on the ground before the day is out. My schoolmate Leithold and I take our positions on the range finder and commence searching the Wiehen Mountain range for possible enemy movements.

As we are scanning the little church at Bergkirchen, on the crest of the range directly to our south, we spot a tank with an unfamiliar silhouette.

The C.O. laughs, saying the target is not at a favorable range, but gives the order to fire one round for the fun of it. As the projectile—our first ever fired at a ground target—makes its way in the direction of the tank ten kilometers away, we strain our eyes through the optics of the range finder. We cannot see an impact.

In the meantime another tank has arrived at the scene. Oblt.

Schrader orders another round fired, again without success. Wachtmeister Buchin, our range finder crew chief, tells us either the projectiles fell short or landed somewhere on the other side of the mountain range. No further rounds are expended.

We hear artillery fire in the distance just as a report is received that a sister battery near the town of Duetzen is under attack. A short time after, a further transmission is received advising they have ceased firing; they are out of action. This places the Allies within six kilometers of Minden and leaves us on the left flank of their thrust toward the Weser River.

Suddenly, at about 10:00 a.m., the sound of tracked vehicles, more like armor, can be heard coming from the direction of the township of Holzhausen II/Brede. Someone shouts, "Herr Oberleutnant, dass muessen die Englaender sein!" It must be the British! A reassuring word comes back telling us, if anything, it's only retreating German forces. The noise of engine motors and the clanging of tank tracks on the pavement gets louder. Suddenly, machine gun fire is coming our way. There, at the edge of the village, a tank is firing on us, moving very slowly out into the open and down the road. The C.O. was wrong. Why doesn't he give orders to open fire?

Our guns are pointing to the sky, all neatly aligned at the proper drill angle. Over there an enemy tank, over here twelve of Germany's dreaded 88s, battle proven and doubling in Russia as antitank weapons, able to tear armor to shreds. But nothing is happening.

Across the field, one of the recently assigned older men from the *Volkssturm* is running away toward the positions of the Italian battery. The German C.O. of that unit reaches for a rifle, aims, fires, and the old man falls. Our first casualty, at the hands of a German officer. We look at each other, fearing what might come next.

The tank rolls slowly along the road spraying our positions with deadly machine gun fire. Our guns are pointing skyward; still no orders to engage the enemy.

An Unteroffizier from the range finder section shouts, "Sauerzapf, Schröder, Laux," and motions for us to join him. We head out in the direction of the gun battery, Laux carrying a Panzerfaust. As we crouch behind the earth mound piled up around our crew quarters, dirt is kicked into my face. The first tank is still firing at us as a second tank comes into sight at the edge of the village. A female communications auxiliarist assigned to the CP overtakes us, runs into the nearest gun emplacement and yells at the boys to ready the gun for firing. We catch up with her just as she is taking aim through the gun barrel. She orders the weapon loaded, and then, "Feuer!" The first round is fired by a woman.

Still no orders from the Command Post, but there is no longer any need for orders.

The boys at the other guns take things into their own hands, lower the barrels and start blasting away, while we continue through the battery area on our way closer to the road. Two planes are circling above. These are not the usual escort planes we have become accustomed to seeing in the sky, like Thunderbolts, Mustangs, or Lightnings. These are Typhoons. We watch them very closely lest they swoop down on us when we are distracted. Just then our four-barrelled machine gun located in the center of the battery area opens fire on the planes. They head off in a westerly direction.

We run into the last gun position before the road just as the second tank passes on its way to Minden. The gun crew members yell at me to get down. In all this excitement I don't know what they are shouting about; all I know is that I'm safe now that I'm inside the parapet. I am standing below the muzzle of their gun, and "boom," they fire over my head at the second tank which has now passed in front of our positions and is nearing the effective range of the Italian gunners down the road. The loud bang takes my hearing away. Disoriented, my ears ringing fiercely, I stagger off to one side.

One of the crew members yells, "Look, the farm house over there, they're showing a white flag."

"Bastards, they surrender while we get killed," shouts the crew chief. "Fire one at the white flag."

A round fired in anger and disillusionment hits the farm house at the edge of the village. Several small three-quarter-ton trucks and a Bren gun carrier have entered upon the highway, large white stars painted on their sides. They are British, a unit of the 6th

Airborne Armoured Reconnaissance Regiment (6 AARR). By now, our 88s are blasting away, ripping them apart. As we leave the safety of the gun emplacement, Laux takes aim with his Panzerfaust and fires.

He yells, "I got him, I got him!"

"Who?" I wonder.

"I hit the front wheel of the motorcycle and the guy went flying through the air!" Laux is overjoyed. The rest of us shake our heads in disbelief that he would waste a Panzerfaust on a single cyclist. A figure clad in khakis and wearing what resembles an American helmet is moving about among the stalled and burning column of vehicles, setting off smoke grenades to obstruct the view of the gunners. Everything on the road seems to be on fire as the 88s keep pouring destruction in that direction.

I turn away, run across the path leading through the battery area to see where the tanks went. I wonder why the soldier on the road would be wearing an American helmet if the unit we were engaging is British. Could we have been misinformed? I run through a small wooden barracks building to get to the other side of the pile of earth that has been placed around it. Inside is another of the old-timers who was just transferred to our unit. He stands there, sad, with his eyes lowered in fear, begging me not to shoot him. As I double-time out the back door, I yell at him to get the hell outside.

I crawl up the dirt mound and look to the southeast. I see the farm where we stored our fuel, coal and brickets for the winter. There, in the hedge, something is moving! I fire a round, my first from the old weapon I was handed just hours ago, and get a good kick in the shoulder. It hurts. I see chickens flying from the hedge and laugh to myself. I fire again; more chickens jump. Guess there aren't any Tommies over there.

We regroup quickly and head for the road on the double, running in a crouched position. All is quiet now; the gunfire is over. The column of trucks is burning, a mass of twisted and torn steel. The two tanks have disappeared in the direction of Minden.

I am in the lead as we approach the road. Just as I prepare to cross over I see an automatic rifle pointing at me and our group. I gasp for what might be my last breath before the hail of bullets knocks me off my feet, and then a young British soldier backs away from his weapon, stands up and raises his hands in surrender. I swallow deeply, suppressing a tear at the turn of events. I feel like I want to thank him, but our uniforms clash and so do our philosophies: we are at war. We look at each other. He must now be wondering if I will honor his sign of surrender. He is young and well dressed. His khaki uniform is neat. I have an urge to speak English, which I speak well, so I ask him whether there are more tanks up the road. Silly question.

A Luftwaffe Sergeant whom I have never seen before pops up out of nowhere; maybe he is from the Italian battery. He tells me he will take the prisoner. I turn around and head up the road toward the smoldering vehicles to catch up with the others. We keep to the ditch at the side of the road in case one of the trucks blows up. We don't know what they are carrying; could be ammunition, fuel or perhaps even demolition explosives. The heat from the fires is sure to set them off, so we'd best proceed with caution. There is debris all over the place. The heavy black smoke smells of burning tires and singed metal. Some of the gun crews are rushing across the field, very few carrying weapons. Everyone wants to see for himself what damage the 88s have done.

We are now on the road, still advancing with caution. Our corporal stops and looks into the ditch to the left. A khaki-clad figure is lying there, face down, with a gashing wound to the back of the head. We hear soft whimpering coming from the motionless body. Help him, somebody; "Sani, Sani," someone shouts; the medic is on his way. I hear a call from the other side of the road and turn. There in the grass is another British soldier. He is lying on his back with both arms and legs stretched out. He looks alright. I tell him in English to get up and I frisk him. I pick up his Sten gun, which looks crudely made, and ask how it works. He says, "You won't need to use it any more." Maybe he's trying to tell me something, but I want to use his weapon instead of the old and antiquated rifle I am now lugging around with me. I point to a latch on the side of the weapon and ask what this is. The safety catch, he says. I try it, it works.

I look around and pick up a pistol before we head for our Command Post. Many more of the boys are making their way to the road to look over the situation. We are now all over the place, walking across the field, laughing, talking with satisfaction and delight of victory over the crack British airborne unit. I sling my rifle and tell the prisoner he can drop his arms if he wishes. He has kept his hands in the air since I told him to get on his feet. He replies he'd like to put his hands behind his neck, but would rather not drop his arms altogether for fear of being shot by someone else. He is right; a prisoner in his situation had best keep his hands away from his body. We walk side by side.

Someone has raised a battle flag at the CP in the meantime. I never even knew we owned one. My POW remarks that we are well dug-in and have pretty good positions. I want so much to converse with him in English but am afraid to talk about our field emplacements, so I just say, "Yes." We make small talk. He remarks about the fluency of my English and asks some questions. I am cautious and hedge my answers.

As we reach the Command Post I spot our Faehnrich, the officer's candidate everyone likes, and decide to turn my prisoner over to him. He loses his temper and control, shouts at the Tommy that he's not a soldier but a gangster and strikes him in the face. I am dumbfounded. I didn't expect this kind of a reaction. The prisoner keeps silent during this outbreak and then moves on to join several other British soldiers standing nearby who were brought in before him. Soon after, my crewmate LWH Leithold is detailed to escort the prisoners to our orderly room in Stemmer. I watch him heading out of our area in the company of a British officer and three enlisted men, all from the motorized column on the road.

After handing the pistol over to Wachtmeister Buchin, I join several of the boys heading back across the field. This time I am carrying a British Sten gun. The boys say that one vehicle near the end of the convoy was abandoned and will be brought to the Command Post. There is talk that one or two enemy trucks that stopped inside the village during our barrage managed to get away. We are puzzled at the small number of prisoners we netted and assume that some of the Tommies probably headed for nearby farms to seek cover when their vehicles were blown out from under them. So we decide on a short foray into the village, now that we have picked up for our own use the weapons the British dropped during the earlier fracas.

After we pass the first houses, I spot a tree along an open section of road and fire a burst into the tree trunk just to try out my new weapon. Perfect. We head for a farmhouse set back from the road, a likely place for someone to take refuge. There are about five or six of us. We search the house from top to bottom, look into closets and even under the beds. All seems in order. Next door is the barn. We look at each other. No one wants to be first through the barn doors. This could be tricky—and dangerous. Suddenly we realize that we are on this excursion on our own, without orders to do what we are doing, so why be heroes? We head back to the battery area.

The captured truck is standing at the Command Post as we return. The C.O. has ordered a scouting mission of the Minden area. He will be accompanied by Oberwachtmeister Bayer who is in charge of the gunnery section, and Wachtmeisters Buchin and Schoenberger, from the range finder crew. In preparation for this mission a pole with a German battle flag attached has been mounted on the side of the truck. It is an odd-looking transport, a khaki vehicle with the white stars on its sides, driven by Germans flying the battle-flag of the Reich.

Before the patrol departs, everyone seems to be crawling all over the vehicle. The Tommies had this three-quarter-ton truck loaded with war souvenirs and booty they picked up along the way. There are German flags of all descriptions, swastika armbands, daggers of various makes and sizes, just about anything a soldier would want to show to his family after the war. We pay little attention to these things, but are interested in the supplies of British cigarettes and snacks that are stashed on the truck as well. I scrounge a camouflaged shelter half and find several packs of the cigarettes.

We receive orders to render the range finder useless. Under no circumstances is this highly sophisticated stereoscopic fire control and directional finder to fall into the hands of the enemy in an operable condition. The *Kommandogeraet* 40 assigned to the 4./434 is a well performing and reliable piece of equipment. It takes the entire crew to lift the four-meter long range finder off the large electromechanical fire control box containing the intricate mechanism. We place it on the ground, take sledgehammers, and batter the stereoscopic eye pieces and other optical fixtures. We then open the housing of the fire control system and damage it severely. This is a sad moment.

After divesting ourselves of our antiaircraft responsibilities, we prepare for the expected return of the enemy by lining up the captured weapons on the parapet of the range finder site, take inventory, and fire a few rounds to familiarize ourselves with the functioning of the British arms now at our disposal. We are generally satisfied with the improved status of our weaponry. If the British decide to come back for a rematch, we will be in a better state of readiness than earlier in the day.

A while later, the C.O. and his patrol return from Minden and the Porta Westfalica. They were able to reconnoiter the highway to the south of the Wiehen Mountains, and they tell of a solid line of Allied armor and vehicles jamming the approaches to Minden. It is apparent that we only met up with an advance patrol or scouting party this morning and that we can expect to be engulfed in a stampede of armor and equipment before long. We are told that Wachtmeister Schoenberger had been hit in the jaw and had to be left behind. This adds another casualty to our list. One of our gunners, a German of Spanish descent, was killed earlier when the tanks peppered our positions with machine gun fire. And there was also the old man who ran when it got rough and was shot by one of our officers.

At approximately 4:00 p.m. a woman on a bicycle approaches our area from the village of Holzhausen II/Brede. I am instructed to ask her to turn back. She reports that British soldiers have entered her village. We allow her to continue on her way to Stemmer and we start paying more attention to the hedges. Something is moving in the bushes. Someone shouts, "There in the tree," but the C.O. is quick to warn us to be sure not to fire on German troops. A single shot is heard; a man is hit in the stomach by a sniper's bullet just ten meters from the CP. He screams in pain and is pulled back into the squad hut from where he was emerging when hit.

Small arms and machine gun fire is now coming in from the

hedges. This is it. We know they are back and duck into our dugout, our weapons ready. Only thirty meters away, our rapid-fire antiaircraft cannon opens up. The gunner blasts the trees and bushes with his 20mm projectiles. Pity the man who gets hit by one of these rounds. There is yelling, it sounds like "Hurray." I look over the parapet and see British paratroopers charging the gun emplacements while firing from the hips with their automatic weapons. They are screaming "Hurrays" as they storm to the top of the parapets, firing without letup. The gunners are surprised, can't raise their heads. The rain of bullets is keeping them low.

There are not too many Tommies, but they are now on top of the emplacements. My classmates and fellow draftees are leaving their dugouts with their hands up in surrender. I can't quite believe that it should end like this. Everything is going so fast.

The gunner of the 20mm rapid-fire gun continues to send spurts of death into the hedges. There, a lone paratrooper charges his position. The gunner gives up—too late. A burst from the trooper's Sten gun hits him before he can get out of his dugout. I am tense; the paratrooper is heading for the range finder position.

He is coming right at me. I aim, ready to pull the trigger—but in the corner of my left eye I see another paratrooper charging from the direction of the 88s, also heading right for the range finder. I think fast, "I get one, the other gets me." A quick calculation, and I dive for the dugout next to the directional finder. My mates Sauerzapf, Laux and Moeser are huddling there dressed in their overcoats. I point to the roof of the dugout, and gesture that the British are above us. We hear shouting, "Come on, come on," and a few bursts from automatic weapons.

I throw my helmet out and clamber to the top of the parapet. Only the two troopers I saw are there, jumping around and firing into the ground. One of our young lieutenants comes up from the communications facility wearing his helmet. This he should not have done; the trooper goes berserk and fires all around him. The Lieutenant falls to his knees begging for mercy while we yell for him to take his helmet off. After he does, the Tommy takes his finger off the trigger. He then yells to the group, "Get a move on, hurry up you dogs," and we are headed for the intersection just behind the first trees at the edge of Holzhausen II/Brede. As we cross the field I empty my pockets, not wanting anything of English origin on me if they decide to search us. We line up three deep when we get to the designated spot.

The paratroopers are frisking some of the men and one or two are punched as English merchandise is yanked from their pockets and thrown in the road. The women auxiliarists are called forward and directed to a farm with orders to remain there through the night. Now the troopers are calling for information on the fate of the prisoners we took earlier in the day. They are irritated and upset and are threatening to shoot us if any harm has been done to their comrades. They threaten to hold back hostages until the prisoners are recovered.

A classmate in the ranks says, "Schröder, sag' den Englaendern doch, dass die Gefangenen in Stemmer sind," tell them the prisoners are in Stemmer. I reply with a curt, "Halt's Maul," shut up.

I have my own problems and worries right now. I am also Walter Schroder, born American from Pawtucket, Rhode Island, and this is not the time to be spouting off in American slang.

2

The Captives

We soon formed a column of threes on orders of the paratroopers and headed west under escort of the crews of the Bren gun carrier and the truck that had managed to escape the devastating fire of our 88s earlier in the day. The British had returned to the scene with reinforcements seasoned in ground combat; we had been no match for them.

Now, just hours after we halted the enemy's advance on Minden with our successful shelling of the armored column, our roles were completely reversed. We were now defeated, captured and trudging along out of step under the watchful eyes of enemy sentinels with automatic weapons. Shouts of "come on" and "move along" left little doubt who was in control. We hurried along in complete silence, passing the barn we had feared to enter earlier, noting the many white flags draped from the windows of the farm houses that lined the road. This was surrender, for real.

No matter what our individual thoughts may have been, no one uttered a word. Our greatest fear was, giving our captors any reason to become irritated. To be certain, we were all wrapped up in our own thoughts, busy sorting out the developments of this day, wary of the uncertainties ahead and wondering what the future—if there were such a thing—might hold. A kilometer or so down the road, we were directed into a fenced area. Discouraged and worn out, we dropped to the ground with a sigh of relief. The grass was cool and refreshing. Sentinels were posted along the perimeter of the pasture. This was to be expected. We didn't care. No one had the drive nor desire to make a run for it. We felt we would be better off to stay put and see what happened next.

Our brief rest ended abruptly when the paratroopers shouted for us to reassemble on the road in marching order. It was getting dark by then and they seemed to be in a hurry. We understood and dashed for the road on the double. Our group was quickly hustled toward the center of Holzhausen II, a village none of us had visited before—strange territory. The column came to a halt. Up front, some of the fellows were being ushered into a barn; could it be they would let us sleep under a roof for the night? A noble thought, but too much to expect. Why would the British want to do this for us?

It soon became clear after the last of us had filed into the barn and the warning was shouted: "There are machine guns at each end of the building. Anyone trying to escape will be shot." They had us right where they wanted us; escape would be fatal to anyone who tried. On the other hand, we had gained the comfort of a night on straw and protection from the chill of the night. The sun had set; it was soon pitch dark around us. No lights, no storytelling or laughing, just quiet. Perhaps a silent prayer here and there. Outside in the night, English voices.

We were up at sunrise. The nightmare had not been a dream— the sentinels were still there. They had slung their weapons over their shoulders nonchalantly and seemed confident as they stood around in the street. The front line must have moved a considerable distance overnight for the few British soldiers watching us to feel so secure.

They supplied us with our first food since being captured. The handful of biscuits and the shared mess kit of tea were gifts from heaven. The biscuits were tasty and made of white flour the likes of which we had not seen since the beginning of the war. The black tea, typically English, was bitter and not to our liking, but we drank it; it warmed our insides.

Soon we had been rounded up and we were off again, marching toward another unknown village. This time I was near the front of the column. Many more prisoners had been rounded up during

the night. Uniforms and insignia of all the services were represented in the endless column of grey as it wound along the country
roads. I looked back. It seemed as though the entire German army
had surrendered. There were many hundreds following each
other. As far as the eye could see, they were coming, all out of
step, some with baggage but most without. Smaller groups were
making their way across open fields to surrender to our escorts.

I finally got up enough nerve to address one of the British
officers in English when I saw he had difficulty making himself
understood to one of the prisoners. After translating his words to
the German, I was asked to remain close to the lead vehicle so I
might translate further orders and pass them on to the senior
officer in the column, who would then relay the information to the
men who followed. After several hours of trekking along secondary
roads in what must have been the hinterlands of the British
advance, for there were few signs of hostile military action, we
reached another peaceful village where we were split up and
assigned to available buildings in smaller groups. During the long
hike some of my classmates from the 4./434th had worked their
way to the front of my column so we could travel in each other's
company rather than get lost among all the strangers. We were
directed into the gymnasium next to the school. The place was
clean and the floor polished. The large windows allowed plenty of
bright daylight to enter the hall.

"Hey, look what's here," one of the boys shouted. A number
of us congregated around him and a pile of wooden crates that
were stacked in the middle of the floor. The markings said it all:
"Panzerfaust," and "Handgranaten." There were bazooka-like antitank weapons in some of the cases and there were a few boxes of
hand grenades. While some of the prisoners were claiming their
territory along the walls of the gym by spreading out what belongings they had been able to salvage before being captured, several
others poked around the crates. "No fuses; can't fire these things,"
they said in disappointment. We looked at each other with raised
eyebrows. I was thinking it was just as well they didn't locate the
firing devices. There would only have been needless slaughter and
some of us among the casualties.

Several of the prisoners were standing near the door asking the sentinel for water and for permission to use the toilet facilities, which had to be entered from outside the gym. I joined their chitchat. The British guard arranged for the canteens to be filled and for those in need to visit the restroom. We laughed out loud when he said they shouldn't try to get away, for there was a machine gun positioned at each of the four corners of the building. He knew we had recognized his bluff; he laughed, too.

The fluency of my English landed me an interpreting assignment across the street from the gym. A British motorcyclist was trying to get a woman to brew him some tea from the contents of a sardine-sized can he was holding. She didn't know what he was saying and couldn't read the words on the can. I was surprised to see that the container had tea, dried milk and sugar in it. All that was needed was to add hot water. I had not seen anything like this before. He soon had his tea and allowed me to satisfy my curiosity by sharing his hot drink with me. It tasted better than expected; very good in fact, especially coming from a Tommy. When he was finished, he gave the woman a can for her own use and drove off. I looked at the woman and she at me, and we both smiled. She went into her house, and I crossed the street back to the gym.

Next, I was asked to translate for a group of British soldiers who were frisking newly arrived Germans on the side of the street. "Tell the Jerries to surrender all pocketknives, cigarette lighters and watches!"

"Watches?"

"They're not supposed to 'ave them!"

I obliged by translating the weird command while the soldiers in khaki proceeded with their collection. I couldn't comprehend why this group was being frisked. None of the others had been.

In a conversation with the guard at the door to the gym I then learned there would be "bully-beef" for rations. I didn't quite know what to make of it, but later on when a can of corned beef and a loaf of white bread were distributed to every three men, I was delighted and knew what the Englishman meant by "bully-beef." I hadn't seen a can of corned beef since I left America, just about eight years before. The odd-shaped cans with keys attached to their tops were exactly as I had known them as a kid. Others nearby mumbled, not knowing for sure what they were eating. I enjoyed the treat from America—the South, to be more accurate. The odd taste of cold, canned corned beef on white bread reminded me of the lunches my mother used to make when I came home from school in New York. I had gotten used to the hard and dark military *Kommissbrot,* but the soft white bread the British supplied in large burlap bags seemed like dessert. I only wished I had some jam.

Our march westward along back roads continued the next morning. Now, for the first time, we saw some real scars of war, evidence of fierce and desperate fighting that must have taken place a few days earlier. Houses were charred and badly damaged by artillery shelling. The roads running through the small farm villages were strewn with debris; roof shingles and broken glass were scattered all over the place. The townspeople had cleared just enough of the roads to allow passage of their horse-drawn wagons, so the crunching of glass under our hobnailed boots could be clearly heard as we made our way through their towns, walking outside the cleared paths. Here and there a curtain was showing through a hole in a wall where once there had been a window frame, and the walls themselves were pockmarked from rifle and machine gun bullets.

Barricades to slow down the advance of the Allies had been erected in just about every village we passed through. In some places these consisted of posts driven into the ground vertically side by side with dirt piled up in back to provide extra strength and support. In other hamlets the barricades were made of old wagons, furniture, bags of sand or piled-up dirt, old doors, just about anything that might slow down men and vehicles. Enemy artillery and armor had wreaked havoc, destroying anything standing in their way. Burned-out charred vehicles of all types and sizes that had been abandoned by our retreating forces and later pushed off the roads were further evidence of the magnitude of the battle that had been fought before giving up the territory and these German towns to the enemy.

We reached a quarry later in the day where we were corralled for another night. As we entered the area, British medics sprayed delousing powder into our trousers and tunics. The menu here consisted of bully-beef, biscuits, a piece of fruit and tea; enough to keep us going. The area was huge and there were German POWs all over the place. Once again, several of us had been able to stay together on the march, so we staked out a place to sleep and then walked around the quarry looking for familiar faces and whatever information we could gather.

During this excursion we picked up an ugly rumor that was particularly upsetting to us. Word was being circulated that minors sixteen years and younger who were found wearing uniforms would be shot. That meant us. I quickly calculated my age and let out a sigh of relief: I had turned seventeen on 30 March, just five days before being captured. The boys who were still sixteen tried hard not to let on that they were scared. I wondered if they would even care if I was seventeen once they started rounding up the young ones. Just the same, I fished through the pockets of my tunic hunting for my papers and checked on my birthdate to be sure it was correct.

We slept on the ground that night, and it was cold. We covered ourselves with our overcoats, but our feet were like ice, almost frozen in our boots when we woke up the next morning. An old-timer told us we should have taken our boots off during the night and slept on them if we were afraid someone might be tempted to make off with them. Perhaps he was right, for it took till noon that day before we warmed up.

Word was out that there would be a hanging and that the senior German officer wanted as many of the prisoners as possible to witness the execution. The accused had been caught stealing from a fellow prisoner during the night. Somehow we didn't say things like "Serves him right." My stomach felt knotted, and I pitied the man. I didn't know him; maybe he was a decorated hero, and maybe not, but what a way for a soldier to die. I thought of the wild west movies I had seen as a boy in America and the way mob justice was doled out to horse thieves. Not one of us joined in watching the public hanging.

Up in the sky about fifty Flying Fortresses were circling and getting into formation. As they flew away toward the east another group assembled, taking off in the same direction. A few days ago our battery would have given them a fiery welcome; now we could only watch as they gathered over German territory and then disappeared in the distance on their way to devastate another one of our cities. Why? As we watched and counted, one of the boys remarked, "It isn't over yet, they say we still have some secret weapons that will be put to use before long."

"It would have to be some sort of devastating miracle weapon to make them turn around now, and they better use it soon," was the reply we heard from one of the others.

Before we settled in for our second night at the quarry we removed our boots as suggested by the soldier earlier in the day. He proved correct, for when we woke up the next morning our feet did not feel cold, and when we put our boots back on after keeping them next to our bodies all night, we felt as good as could be expected.

This morning's rumors had it that we, the minors, would be discharged and sent home. We grasped at the encouraging news and quickly made direct inquiries with one of the British officers. He dismissed the information as incorrect and reminded us that the war was still going on. He was perfectly right; we just kept reaching for any and every straw that might hold hope of improving our lot. At least this rumor sounded better than what we had heard the day before, so we weren't terribly disappointed. He had been polite about it when he gave us the negative response, almost as though he was sorry he couldn't oblige and send us home. It probably wouldn't have worked out too well anyway, since most of our homes were in the central part of the Reich and still under German control.

Sometime before noon the prisoners were moved out of the quarry on foot in groups of several hundred. When we reached the road, a line of trucks was waiting for us. We were directed to mount up and very quickly dashed for empty seats in the cargo area. Those who missed out on a seat held on to the tarpaulin supports and remained standing, just like the guards, who had been assigned one to the rear of each truck while another stood on the front seat next to the driver. This was our first chance to get a close look at one of their trucks. What interested me was the circular steel ring above the seat next to the driver, which the guard explained was a mount for a machine gun. As I scanned the area quickly I noticed several trucks that indeed had machine guns attached to the circular steel rings. I thought that was a nifty idea. The gunner could fire at targets in the air as well as on the ground, and in all directions. Standing on top of the front seat had some advantages, but also some distinct disadvantages, particularly under fire.

The motors were started and our line of trucks was set in motion, heading west. Before long we were on a main artery, definitely a lifeline for the advancing enemy, for the road was crammed with vehicles of all types and sizes, all heading east into the heart of Germany. Every now and then our trucks had to hug the edges of the highway to make way for a column of tanks and other heavy equipment that took up more than half the width of the road. Then there were trucks and more trucks, all loaded down with troops, equipment or supplies, also men in jeeps, on motorcycles and even riding bicycles. Here and there we saw an accident or breakdown, occasionally an ambulance, and now and then a wrecker busy moving an idle piece of machinery. Along the way the ditches and the edges of the road were littered with individual equipment discarded by retreating German troops. Abandoned artillery pieces and tanks had been pushed off the road in some places, while in others similar equipment had been used to the very end as evidenced by the bullet holes in the charred remains of motor vehicles turned over or lying on their sides, tires burned.

The convoy rolled through towns and hamlets; there was hardly a place where the war had not left its mark. It was sad to witness the aftermath of the many smaller battles that took place in and around the settlements and in the fields along the line of the Allied advance. The sight of an occasional wooden cross adorned with a German helmet next to a mound of dirt made us realize how lucky we were to still be alive. The men on the trucks began to sing; Germans always sing. But their tunes were subdued; instead of marching or victory songs, they sang of leaving their loved ones behind, and of shedding tears. "Moecht' im Stillen heisse Traenen weinen, als ich Abschied nahm von ihrer Hand." And then there was the World War I song of the hills of Sedan and the infantry soldier standing watch next to his fallen comrade killed by the enemy's bullet. The songs were mournful expressions of disillusioned men, disappointed and hopeless.

It had become very clear during the last few hours, after witnessing the steady and uninterrupted flow of men and materials coming from the west, that the Reich's existence for all practical purposes was doomed. The unopposed stream of heavy combat equipment heading deeper into Germany on the main roads coupled with the continued and incessant bombings from the air forced us to realize what none of us a short time ago had considered possible, namely that Germany could lose the war after all. No one had even wanted to think of such an outcome; that would have been treason. Until now, even with the serious setbacks suffered in Russia and on the Allied fronts, we had believed in ultimate victory. But seeing is believing, and from what we were seeing, things were not very encouraging.

The road took a turn near a small patch of trees, and just as we were coming around the bend we could see two abandoned German tanks buried in the ground, with only their turrets showing. It gave the appearance of a strong point, two small fortresses, or a site for an ambush. I wondered why they had covered such powerful tanks, thereby immobilizing them from further movement. I soon learned from one of the prisoners that the shortage of fuel necessitated digging in the tanks at strategic points, and also that this was not the only such site. That may have been the right answer, but these tanks had not seen any action. They seemed to be in perfect condition, ready for battle, but for their missing crews.

Later in the day while rolling past a marshalling yard somewhere in the vicinity of Ibbenbueren-Rheine, we saw many more tanks and vehicles still on railcars. Perhaps the tracks had been bombed or the locomotives shot up by Allied fighter planes, preventing the trains from making their deliveries in time to help the German efforts. For the trains and equipment stranded here, this yard had become the end of the line.

After traveling the busy highways for most of the day our convoy pulled off the main road and followed less congested secondary routes until we reached a temporary P.W. cage near a wooded area. The first thing after dismounting and before filing into the compound was for us to receive another dose of DDT powder up our sleeves and into our trousers. I thought if they kept this up without giving us a chance to wash, the smelly powder would soon stick to our skin and become crusty. Inside the compound we received the usual crackers, bully-beef and tea. By now the bully-beef fare was becoming monotonous and dull. The thrill experienced a few days ago at the canned beef taste was wearing off.

While sitting in the grass I noticed several of the prisoners digging small holes with their empty corned beef cans. After observing them for a while I noticed they were scooping water from the holes. To satisfy my curiosity I inquired what they were doing. They showed me that ground water very quickly filled up a hole just ten to fifteen centimeters deep and when the sediment had settled the water was paletable, cool and clear enough to drink right from the ground. I went back to my place and tried it for myself. To my delight it also worked for me. After quenching my thirst I collected another can full and rinsed my face and hands for the first time in days. It was very refreshing but no substitute for a good scrubbing.

When it was dusk I watched the bartering that was going on between the British and the Germans. I couldn't comprehend how or why one would trust the other, but here, to my amazement, the prisoners were throwing their watches over the barbed wire fence to the Tommies, who caught them, assessed their value and made their offers in terms of packs of cigarettes. For the most part a quantity of cigarettes would be agreed to, some times as much as a whole paper bag full. I soon learned that the number of diamonds in the movement of the watch determined the value the buyer attached to the timepiece. When a deal couldn't be made the watch would be thrown back over the fence. At first I couldn't believe that this was really happening. I was sure some foolish P.W. would lose his watch with nothing to show for it, but I was wrong. The Tommies always kept their word.

When I finally curled up on the ground for another night in the open, I wondered why we were at war. The fellows on the other side were no different from us. Given a chance we might even be able to get along with each other. The way they spoke English made them seem stuck-up and superior, but I realized that was superficial. Maybe they really were high-and-mighty, but from what I had seen so far, they seemed OK.

The next morning we were back on the trucks and once again a part of the mass movement of men and materials on the highways of northwestern Germany, heading still farther away from the fighting. Our travels were never monotonous for there was always something new to be seen, and not just scenery. Once I saw a lone jet-powered German aircraft in the sky. What was he doing? Maybe taking aerial photos of the Allied columns in anticipation of a counter-blow? The guards didn't pay much attention to the plane, but we wondered if this was all the Luftwaffe was able to muster these days. This was one of the newly developed German jet planes. We had been well trained to identify all types of aircraft with precision and accuracy, but we couldn't place this one. We never did find out what it was.

Our convoy continued westward without any holdups except for an occasional stop so we could relieve ourselves. After spending another night in a makeshift P.W. receiving facility with repeats of cold food (but this time with the slight variation of added cheese, and also the longed-for jam, but more of the black tea), we were off once again, aboard trucks, this time following the road from Rheine enroute to Wesel.

About a month previously we had heard of the massive Allied air-landing and parachute operation that had taken place near the town of Wesel on our side of the Rhein. Before that, we had seen pictures in newspapers showing the preparations that were being made in that same area in anticipation of just such an assault from the air. I remembered seeing a photo of wooden poles driven into the ground at angles to rip the bottoms out of gliders during any attempted airlanding operation. We had felt very confident about these defensive countermeasures at the time. Now I wondered. After all, the Allies had succeeded and were moving ever deeper inland at a frightening pace even as we were being moved farther away from the battle zone.

The massive paratroop and airlanding operation concentrated on Wesel had involved over 21,000 personnel, shuttled in from airfields in England and France by an armada of several thousand transport planes and gliders escorted by yet another thousand fighter planes. That was on 24 March. In less than two weeks they had managed to subdue the German forces in the landing area and had advanced more than 150 kilometers into German territory, smashing any resistance in their path. Now, traveling through Wesel we were seeing the results of this operation.

We could tell that the fighting had been fierce. The damage we had observed during the last few days was dwarfed by the magnitude of the destruction we were now witnessing. As we drew closer to the Wesel landing and drop zones we could see places that had been literally flattened, with nothing left but mounds of rubble. Among piles of burnt wood and twisted steel were the charred carcasses and pitiful remains of war implements and equipment. We passed a landing zone, an open field littered with the blackened hulks of gliders hit by groundfire. And then there were the remains of cargo aircraft that had either crash-landed or were brought down by German antiaircraft fire. Next to these silent remains were the graves of Allied paratroopers, their helmets sitting atop makeshift wooden crosses right where they had died. We fell into silence. Even the singing came to an abrupt end as we realized we were not unique in our misery.

The convoy entered a marshalling yard not far from Wesel where we were transferred to cattle cars in a waiting train. According to rumors we were to be shipped to Antwerp to participate in the reconstruction of the damaged port facilities. It looked like our days of relaxation would be coming to an end. We were crowded into the cars standing up with hardly enough room to breath. The doors slammed shut and soon the train was steaming westward. It was extremely difficult to find a way to sit and try to relax. Loud curses could be heard as men were stepped on by others making their way to one of the corners of the wagon to relieve themselves.

The train shook and rattled along the bumpy tracks for hours on end. We knew we were in for trying times.

A few of the men kept a steady vigil peering through the cracks and spaces between the boards in the sides of the car as we chugged along, deeper into strange territory, past villages and terrain no one really knew. From their descriptions, we were travelling in a westerly direction somewhere in the border region of Holland and Belgium. This checked with earlier rumors that we would be used to clean up the rubble in the harbor district and city of Antwerp. Recalling that this port city so vital to the Allies had been under fire of our V1 and V2 rockets, we knew the damage must have been considerable and that it now would take an army to clean up the mess. Maybe the rocket trails we observed through our range finder optics from time to time were from V2s targeted for Antwerp and not England as we thought at the time. Who knows? It didn't really matter much any more.

I felt sorry for myself. I was filthy. The delousing powder had formed crusty spots on my body and there was no way to wash and clean up. We were lucky to get a sip of water to drink. And then, there was that offensive smell of heavy odor from perspiration to which all our sweaty bodies contributed. Being hemmed in as we were didn't help the situation. My stomach finally turned and I got the dry heaves when a fellow next to me pulled off his jack boots. The sickening stench of his sweaty woollen socks had done it. To top it off, my ears were still ringing from that gun blast several days before. The loud high-pitched sound was very annoying. How I wished it would go away. What a mess I was in, I thought, and I pitied myself being in this predicament with no way out. I felt lost and completely discouraged. To make matters even worse, I no longer saw any of my schoolmates who had served with me in my flak unit; I was alone among all these strangers. My comrades may have been in the same car with me, but I didn't see any of them. Few of the men around me were talking. Most sat silently, staring into nowhere with sullen expressions on their faces, wrapped up in their inner thoughts. I know I was.

The bumpy and shaky journey continued as it began to turn dark outside. After maneuvering a while for some elbowroom, I was finally able to squeeze my feet and legs between other stretched-out bodies and get into a position so I might fall asleep and for a time forget the plight I was in. But I couldn't sleep. I was too restless; my mind was still wide awake and hard at work. I just lay there, eyes closed, trying to doze off. Instead, I kept thinking of the past and some of the good times I had had as a kid in America. I kept asking myself how I had ever gotten into this situation. Every so often I gained control of myself and shook my head just to rid myself of these seditious thoughts, hoping I had not dozed off and broadcast my inner feelings to an audience of complete strangers. Although we were prisoners, we were still soldiers of the Reich. Battles may have been lost, but the war was still raging, and far from being over. Any utterances of my most intimate thoughts could prove fatal if overheard by the wrong person.

I must have dozed off after all, for suddenly there were train whistles, brakes were screeching, the cars were being bumped along the tracks and across switches while the locomotive was blowing off steam. The train came to a stop. The shaking up we received was enough to awaken anyone from whatever his dreams or thoughts might have been. We were quickly brought back to the reality when the doors to the cattle cars opened. Bright spotlights were trained in our direction, shining directly in our eyes and blinding us momentarily. Guards in British uniforms, some armed with rifles and fixed bayonets, others with Sten guns, and a few with billy clubs, were standing on the platform yelling hoarsly, "Come on" and "Let's go," while a throng of jeering civilians lined the edge of the platform, shouting and screaming. Some were shaking their fists at us while others were angrily waving sticks above their heads. We couldn't believe our eyes and dreaded having to leave the safety of the cattle car to face the vicious crowd and the shouting guard contingent. The station sign read: La Hulpe.

3

Camp 2228

The cars were quickly emptied of the prisoners as the guards pushed and shoved the men along the platform. Now it was our turn. Standing in the car door, I glanced briefly at the restless crowd outside. I was squinting. The bright station lights were shining right at me. The throng of civilians on the opposite side of the tracks was in a frenzy, yelling and screaming. Among all the shouting I was certain I heard the word "bosh" again and again. I hesitated before leaping to the ground. My feet felt heavy; I was scared, more afraid of this unruly crowd than when I'd been under direct enemy fire a few days before. I could see British soldiers wearing tams among the many helmeted sentinels on the platform who had formed a cordon between the prisoners and the civilian mob. Trusting the Tommies would keep things under control, I took a deep breath and jumped. My feet were on Belgian soil for the first time in my life; the circumstances could not have been any worse.

Quickly I elbowed and squeezed my way to the center of the hundreds of POWs mulling around the platform. They were forming up into marching order in ranks six or seven abreast. I claimed and held a place in the second row from the left when we were ordered, around midnight, to move out. At least I was not in the outside row, subjected to angry civilians shaking fists and sticks. Sleepy and worn out, we dragged our feet as we trudged along under the watchful eyes of the guards, who had increased their shouting of "*Schnell, schnell.*" They were pushy, jabbing men in the ribs with the muzzles of their rifles or the Sten guns they were carrying.

They were a bunch of rowdy troops. There was something about them that wasn't English. They seemed shorter than most British soldiers I had seen so far and their uniform gear was somewhat different. They were equipped with leather gaiters and belts, while the Tommies wore heavy webbing. We soon sorted out that the helmeted sentinels were Belgians. Another giveaway was that the Tommies were yelling "Come on" and "Get a move on," while the helmeted troops were shouting "*Schnell, schnell.*" That was German, but could also have been Flemish. I wondered where the Belgians had come from; Belgium didn't have an army while under German occupation and the Allies had been back only a short time. Most of the soldiers were very young. Perhaps they were recent recruits or volunteers. It seemed they were trying to impress their countrymen and the British provost staff with their tough demeanor.

When the column began to move toward the end of the platform, the civilians along the route struck the passing POWs with clubs and sticks. A woman hit one of the men behind me with an umbrella. He was pushed by a guard at the same time and fell to the pavement. I couldn't tell if others got him back on his feet as the column kept moving ahead like a steamroller.

The crowd thinned out as we reached the end of the platform, but even before we cleared the depot area we were being hustled along in double time. I felt shaky and weak, but I had to run; I didn't want to fall, not now. I suppressed my tears. Glassy-eyed, I kept up with the men around me until permitted to slow down to a marching pace, or something like it. We were all out of step by then, but the going was a bit easier. Still, they kept us moving along at a steady pace in the dark, first through the town and then along an open country road. The trek seemed endless. Every step seemed to drain the last bit of energy out of my system. There was no stopping, we had to keep going. To falter could be disastrous and bring the wrath of some angry guard upon us. There in the distance, not too far away anymore, was a wide area all lit up. It seemed we were heading for daylight; hopefully, it was our destination.

Commands were shouted in English to get in proper marching order, six abreast. We pulled ourselves together the best we could under the circumstances and headed into the glare of spotlights that were trained in our direction. There was high barbed wire fencing on both sides of the road with lights mounted on top. We entered the enclosure through a large gate. We stumbled forward with a sigh of relief, to find we had only reached the main thoroughfare of a very large, fenced-in enclave. We kept moving along the pavement at a fast pace, with British provost guards urging us to move along, and the usual shouts of "Come on, come on." The night was pitch black all around us; we saw nothing but barbed wire lit up by lights spaced every few meters. Now and then we could make out a watchtower with a searchlight in the distance. An eerie feeling of uneasiness came over me, and I was afraid of the unknown, of what might be waiting for us in the darkness behind the lights.

Finally the column slowed down. We stretched our necks to see what was going on up front. Ranks of prisoners, six abreast, were being ushered through a gate to the left of the road. Soon it was our turn. A simple sign fastened to the fence at that point read: "5." Across the street to our right I could see a sign with the number "18" painted on it. When our escorts had assured themselves of the body count we were double-timed through the gate. Beyond, we were again in complete darkness with only the fence lights to mark off the boundaries of our new world. Without urging, we quickly fell out of ranks, relieved and thankful to have made it through this ordeal. As I walked deeper into the dimly lit darkness of this strange yet welcome sanctuary, I dropped to the ground, exhausted. The dampness and the fresh smell of clover were all I needed to fall into a deep sleep.

It was dawn and the beginning of a new day when I awoke in my bed of clover. I lay on my back and contemplated the clouds in the sky. What beauty! I turned my head to the left. I saw a high barbed wire fence and a tower; I turned my head to the right, and saw another barbed wire fence and a tower. I sat up. What in the world. . . ? Just twenty meters away there were rows of tents, some round, some oblong. Had I only walked a few more meters last night, I'd have come upon them. Lucky it hadn't rained. From what I could see, I was not the only one who had dropped into the clover and stayed there for the night. All around me men were stretching and checking whatever gear they had managed to bring with them. I was hungry. An elderly soldier sitting in the grass near me opened his satchel and pulled out a whole salami. He cut a hunk off for himself, saw me watching, cut another piece and handed it to me. I was puzzled but very thankful that he would share his most precious possession—food—with me, at a time when he knew he could not replenish his treasure. He smiled and told me to enjoy it. I did.

I felt much better with something in my stomach. I stood up and looked all around hoping to spot one of the kids from my school and Flak-Batterie. I didn't see anyone who looked familiar, so I set out for a walk through the tent area to look for my friends and also to find a tent where I might be able to settle in. It wasn't too long before I located several of my classmates and their tent, where I too could stay. Together we scouted out *Lager* 5. We found the washing facilities the British called ablutions. These consisted of long metal troughs with water pipes running their entire length, all set up under a sheet-metal sunroof. Just what we needed: a good washing up! No soap, no towels, who cared? We stripped, and cupping our hands, we filled them with water and washed up at last. The cold water felt good. I felt invigorated, refreshed, more like the real me.

After the make-shift bath, I heard shouts from across the field calling for a *Dolmetscher*, an interpreter, to come forward. Near the gate I could see several British officers and a German senior sergeant trying to converse. I made a wild dash across the field of clover, leaving my classmates behind. An Unteroffizier had reached the group before me and was already interpreting for the British by the time I arrived, short of breath. The senior sergeant asked what I wanted and I replied I was answering the call for an interpreter. He looked at me as though he couldn't quite believe I could do the translating. From his facial expressions it seemed he was about to dismiss me, when one of the British officers said to the other, "I wonder what he wants."

I quickly responded, in English, "Sir, I heard your call for an interpreter, so I came up to the gate. Can I be of any help to you gentlemen?"

The officers looked at each other, somewhat puzzled. One said in a subdued voice, "This lad sounds like a bloody Yank."

It didn't take much more. From that moment on, I was the interpreter to Wachtmeister Foltz, the Lagerfuehrer of Compound 5. The job required that I remain near the gate at all times so I would be available to translate whenever members of the British staff visited our compound. The pace was very hectic, especially during the first few days, as much had to be done to get organized. We needed an accurate count of the prisoners to justify and requisition the needed food supplies for the men. The first order of business was therefore to assemble the prisoners for a head-count. With typical German military precision, the troops quickly lined up in the field, trampling the clover into the ground. We formed units of 100, twenty abreast and five deep. The provost guard and Lagerfuehrer took the count while I followed with pad and pencil, checking the accuracy of their figures. All worked out well. The first head-count agreed with the number of men that had been logged into the enclosure during the night.

Next, the cookhouse had to be made operational. There were close to 3,000 hungry POWs gathered in the field and in the tents, waiting to be fed. The messing facility was geared to burning coal, but oil was more plentiful, the British said. While a team of cooks went to work trying their hand at brewing black tea and the first cauldrons of hot coffee (real coffee, not the Ersatz everyone was used to), an engineer from the University of Heidelberg rounded up a group of volunteers to help plan the conversion of the stoves from coal to oil.

The group soon began collecting empty metal biscuit containers to be cut up and formed into the tubing needed to direct the flow of the oil, while carvers went to work making the wooden spigots that would be attached to the tubing to control the flow. The project required the full cooperation of the British guard contingent, especially since we needed metal shears, which were the ideal tool to cut barbed wire, along with several mallets and some heavy steel sheets from which the oil pans would be cut and formed. The conversion was a very slow and tedious process that took several weeks. Every evening the tools were counted and returned to the provost guard shack outside the gate to the compound.

Once the job was done, our cookhouse became the showplace of Camp 2228. We in Compound 5 had come up with a first, and the British were truly amazed. I was kept busy giving tours of our messing facilities to their senior officers (including several brigadiers), explaining to them what our men had done. A passing remark from one of the visiting officers said it all: "Give those bloody Jerries some tin cans and a mallet and they'll come out in a tank." His off the cuff statement was an open acknowledgement that they respected our accomplishment despite their generally cold and snobbish attitude.

This accomplishment was particularly impressive considering that Compound 5 was just a small segment of the overall Camp 2228 complex, which occupied some 200 hectares of farmland along the road from Overijse to Terlanen. Intended to accommodate 60,000 captives, the camp was divided into twenty smaller compounds with a capacity for up to 3,000 prisoners each. As soon as the British had assessed the benefits of our coal to oil boiler conversion, they arranged for the camp leaders of the other occupied P.W. compounds to visit and view our oil-operated messing facility, all in preparation for additional conversions, which were implemented shortly thereafter.

Daily deliveries of white bread and other food supplies were made to our commissary store room, a Nissen hut located immediately inside the gate. From there, the dry food was doled out to representatives of each unit of 100. Because of a shortage of space, up to sixteen men were assigned to a tent normally intended for eight. A 100-man unit thus comprised the men in six or seven tents. For administrative and control purposes the tents were numbered and rosters established listing the names of the men assigned to each. Whenever someone was transferred to the sick bay in another Nissen hut near the gate, or to the camp hospital outside the compound, the rations needed to be adjusted. Warm meals were dished out to each man directly at the cookhouse, where three sittings per meal were required to accommodate our

3,000 people. The variety of fresh vegetables and other staple foods supplied made it necessary to adopt an *Eintopf* menu, one that allowed for bulk one-pot cooking, like soups and stews.

During the early days of our confinement our food allocation was sufficient and of such quality and variety to make us realize that our submarine strikes against Allied ships and convoys had ultimately not caused the critical shortages we had expected. As long as they could feed their prisoners so well, they couldn't be hurting. The situation changed markedly, however, when Germany surrendered unconditionally on 7 May, ending the war. Not only were we suffering the humiliation of total defeat, but we were now at the complete mercy of our captors.

Our precarious situation was compounded further when news of heinous crimes and atrocities reportedly committed by Germans against concentration camp inmates in unheard-of places like Belsen and Dachau were made known to the world. As an interpreter working closely with the British, I was among the first to hear of these crimes. It was hard to believe the stories at first; it was almost impossible for such things to happen. However, after reading English newspapers and seeing first-hand photos in magazines, I had to admit to myself that the unthinkable and unbelievable had indeed happened. I felt ashamed to be a German. My stomach turned at the mere thought of the cruelty with which some of our people had treated the concentration camp inmates. We, all of us, the prisoners of war, were the most logical objects of blame in a new wave of resentment. This was manifest in the almost immediate curtailment of rations across the board, and in a much tougher attitude on part of the British and Belgian guards.

Some of the more enterprising prisoners had managed to scrounge cardboard; which they spread on the floor of their tents so they wouldn't have to sleep on bare ground and risk illness. This was considered unauthorized contraband, and the cardboard had to be surrendered as part of a campaign of subtle retaliation and chicanery. On the other hand, supplies of shoes, some blankets and even uniform pieces were made available for those in dire need of such items, and there were many in need. I picked out a brand new pair of laced boots with a label that read: "Made in U.S.A." They were very much like the ones I had had as a kid in

New York, real American boots with a moccasin cut. I appraised them carefully. They were beautiful. Deep within me I felt American.

The uniforms supplied were British khaki, with holes cut in the backs of the jackets and in the legs of the trousers that had been covered with bright round patches of yellow—perfect for a guard to aim at should the wearer try to make a run for it. I was well acquainted with our supply sergeant by then. He allowed me to rummage through the shipment of clothes at my leisure before distribution was made to the others. Among the bundles of khaki trousers I found a pair that fit me just right, and, best of all, someone had forgotten to cut the hole above the knee. Perfect. I tore off the yellow patch and swapped the khaki pants for my blue-grey Luftwaffe trousers, which had a tear in them.

The YMCA had shipped in a few items of sports gear, several musical instruments, and also some books, among them a few volumes in English. The supply sergeant suggested I see if there was anything I might want before he made a general distribution. I couldn't believe my eyes; there, on the floor of the big supply tent, in the middle of nowhere, was *Huckleberry Finn*. I had read this story as a boy in America; how I wanted to read it again! He observed my excitement as I thumbed through the book and he told me to take it. I did, and headed for my tent. It was near the gate, among several others in which our orderly room, the Lager-fuehrer, the supply sergeant, the commissary NCO and the company clerk were housed.

Being on the camp staff had its advantages. Rudi, our carpenter, made a few bunks from scrap wood and burlap bags at the request of Lagerfuehrer Foltz. After the older men had received theirs, I too was given a bunk of my own, which was a real status symbol. I did not accept this privilege without payment, however. Our NCOs were forever trying to chisel the cigarettes from me that an occasional good-hearted British officer or provost guard would give to me. That was fine, since I didn't smoke, and I quickly learned that cigarettes were like money; one needed cigarettes to barter. Men were depriving themselves of their food rations, just for a smoke. It was sad to see once-proud soldiers diving for a cigarette butt flipped on the ground by a passing guard. I was able to pay for my bunk in this manner, or at least show my appreciation. One day, a tailor made a cap for me from camouflage tent material, shaped like the headgear worn by the Afrika Korps. I had always wanted one like it; now, as a POW, I finally had one.

With several thousand men crisscrossing the cloverfield all day long on their way back and forth to the kitchen, the ablutions, the latrines, the supply tent, and the twice-daily headcounts, not to mention the ballgames that were played in the same area, the beautiful groundcover of clover disappeared quickly. After the first heavy spring rain we were trudging through mud flats, dark and soggy muck. The ground was rich, dark farm soil. When it got soaked by the rain, our feet sank into it right up to our ankles. Something had to be done to stabilize the ground, especially near the gate, and on the more frequently traveled routes between the administrative area, the sick bay, and the commissary store.

It was decided to pave several walks by filling empty vegetable cans with sand and standing them on end, side by side like cobblestones. The British approved the idea and came up with several loads of sand. They also arranged for the pickup of empty tin cans from the adjacent enclosures. We at Compound 5 were at it again, improving our lot with another self-help project while at the same time giving some of the men an opportunity to do something constructive. Up till now they had just been sitting around, bored, doing little or nothing, perhaps worrying what things were like back home, if they still had a home.

As part of the paving project, I suggested building a monument in the center of the field, which would honor the men who had lost their lives fighting for their country, and, at the same time, would reduce the area to be paved. The suggestion was accepted and a plan was drawn up for a low-profiled memorial including sculptures of both German and British helmets. One of the British sentinels offered his own helmet as a model. The monument turned out to be another masterpiece, the work of a few skilled artisans. Everyone seemed elated that we had broken the ice, having tackled the project in cooperation with the British. We knew the word would get out and make its way all the way up to the commandant, Colonel King. Major Powel, his deputy, had visited our compound regularly before.

We enjoyed the artwork and the accomplishment for several days, until early one morning a report was made that the British helmet had been destroyed. We of the camp staff were aghast. The gate guards were furious; they felt insulted and humiliated. Had he been caught, the perpetrator would undoubtedly not have fared too well with the British. Though very disappointed, the British swallowed their pride and refrained from any form of retaliation. Under the circumstances we could only apologize to the guard contingent and relay to our fellow POWs during the headcount that morning our own resentment of those we called the "cowards of the night." Rather than attempting to sculpt another British helmet and running the risk of having some fanatic destroy it again, the staff decided it would be more appropriate to remove the sculpture of the German helmet as well. It seemed the only sensible thing to do. The dedication memorializing the fallen of World War II remained as originally set down.

Men with critical skills as stevedores, bricklayers and steel workers were called up and shipped back to Germany soon after the cessation of hostilities, to help in the reconstruction of essential facilities and to support the occupying forces and the civilian population. Lagerfuehrer Foltz left with one of the first groups of repatriates, and Oberwachtmeister Karl Rehfeld, a former border official, assumed the position. The vacant spaces were quickly filled from among new arrivals. Several times, groups of German officers were put up in our compound for short periods, until they could be transferred to an officers' camp.

One of these officers, a young SS Lieutenant, told us that his unit was in the immediate vicinity of my gun battery on 4 April, the day we were captured. His men were in the village of Stemmer, with orders to provide infantry support and cover for our 88s. Just as they were leaving the settlement to cross the fields on their way to our positions, however, they heard gunfire and saw us being hustled from our emplacements by British paratroopers. The Lieutenant noted that the British attack appeared swift and effective. His SS Detachment was too far away to intervene, in any case.

That night they observed from a distance as our shelters were torched. The next day they too were captured. That night I thought what might have happened had the SS men arrived in our battery area before the paratroopers charged our positions. Perhaps we would have been able to hold out another few hours, or even a day, but in the end we would have been flushed out, and with even greater casualties. It was perhaps best that it had happened as it did.

Among the new arrivals at Compound 5 were troops that had never been captured; troops that had been in Denmark and in Schleswig-Holstein with Admiral Doenitz until the end, when they were interned. These troops had been allowed to carry their sidearms and had continued to maintain discipline within their original organizations even after the unconditional surrender. They were disgruntled when required to turn in their weapons and face the same conditions as all the other prisoners of war. Some had hoped, in the early days after the cessation of hostilities, to be integrated into British units in the event the Allies should break with the Soviets and launch a drive toward Russia. There was a lot of wishful thinking at the time. When they arrived at our camp they insisted they were internees, not POWs, but they found out the hard way that they would be treated no differently than the thousands who had already spent weeks in the mud of Camp 2228.

Life for the camp staff was hectic during the summer of 1945; our camp population was constantly changing as some men were repatriated and others arrived. The pace of the turnover kept hopes—but also tempers—high. The British would show up at the gate with a roster of men to be shipped out and demand they be ready posthaste. There certainly was no difficulty involved in packing; hardly anyone had any possessions of any significance, save a blanket perhaps and maybe a satchel with a few pieces of clothing. The difficult part of the whole thing was to find the men; they might be in the compound if they weren't in their tents. And spotting the transferees took the staff members away from their normal duties.

One day as I was being badgered by a Scottish sergeant to get a group of men together, an antiaircraft auxiliarist, a Luftwaffenhelfer like myself, came up to me and asked if he could help me out as an interpreter. He spoke perfect English, unmistakably American. He told me he had been born in Milwaukee. His story paralleled mine very closely, in fact. His name was Irving. I accepted his offer of help and he was of great assistance during those pressure-filled days. Despite the stress we were under, I couldn't help laughing openly when he opened his mouth and spoke with that Yankee slang, just too perfect for a German. It was obvious he had been in America; the slang he used could not have been acquired in a German school, that was for sure.

One day the Scottish sergeant came tearing into our compound again, yelling for me, *"Dolmetscher, Dolmetscher!"* I ran to the gate to meet him. I was afraid of him; he was a member of the Detention Camp staff. I often saw him being given a ride up the main camp street in a wheelbarrow, pushed by some unlucky prisoner with a shaven head and the striped suit of a convicted criminal, or concentration camp inmate. Whenever the sergeant came to our compound he ranted and raved, threatening to send me to the Detention Camp if I did not get the prisoners he wanted ready in the few minutes he gave me. He always seemed in a hurry. This day he stood waiting, legs astride and a swagger stick in one hand grinning broadly so all his large teeth showed. His tam sat at a cocky angle on one side of his head. "Dolmetscher, get the men on parade, I have a list of fifty who will be transferred. I'll give you ten minutes to get the men in formation." He wanted close to 3,000 men lined up in ten minutes, no matter where they were or what they were doing. This included cooks, medics, people washing or on the latrines, no matter; everyone on parade—or else.

The sergeant began yelling again, and he pushed me. Lager-fuehrer Rehfeld had heard the commotion and came our way, his face red and his bald head shining as though the skin had been stretched to maximum capacity. He was ready to explode. I told him quickly what had happened and that we had to get the troops lined up in minutes. Our tinsmith had made a giant megaphone, so large that it had to be supported by a permanent tripod. This device was used to wake the men in the morning, but also to call it a day at 10:00 at night. Rehfeld went to the megaphone and bellowed his orders for an immediate assembly of all personnel on the parade ground, without exception. His assistant double-timed up and down the rows of tents shouting similar commands while the NCOs in charge of the 100-man units were rushing their men along. Compound 5 was on parade as demanded. Roughly twenty-eight units of 100 men each were aligned around the ball field, all standing at attention as the Scottish sergeant walked to the center of the field accompanied by the Lagerfuehrer and myself.

The sergeant commenced calling out the names of the prisoners he wanted to assemble in a group in the center of the field. They were not moving fast enough for him and he began kicking and pushing them, shouting at them to get a move on. Next he struck out with his swagger stick. He was working himself into a frenzy. His actions were inexcusable. As I looked across the field I noticed one unit of 100 SS men slowly moving forward on a solid front twenty abreast, taking small but deliberate steps. The sergeant had not noticed and continued with his antics while the block of SS men took a few more steps forward. It was very evident at this point that the unit was no longer aligned with the others, and had advanced several meters toward the center of the field. The sergeant finally noticed. At first he only waved at them to go back, but then he drew his pistol and started waving it above his head, threatened to shoot anyone who came near.

I could see a disaster in the making. "I'll tell them to get back," I told him, "but you best holster your pistol." Then I walked over to the SS unit and told them it wasn't worth getting killed on account of one crazy Scot. Besides, even if they could overwhelm him, there were still the trigger-happy Belgians with their machine guns in the towers overlooking the compound.

Not long before, a German prisoner had been shot by one of the Belgians, right out from under the watchful eyes of his British escort. He had been mending the fence in the forbidden neutral zone, a ten meter-wide strip in front of the high barbed wire fence. After that the term neutral zone faded from our vocabulary and it became known as the death zone instead. Even the British had been angry then at the "good-for-nothing Belgiques."

Reminding the troops of this incident worked; the SS men, who had locked arms in the meantime, began to back up. The sergeant calmed down, finally got the fifty men he came for, gave them fifteen minutes to get their things, and then headed them out the gate. Not another word was said about the fracas.

This episode changed the Scotsman's attitude, however. From then on, he was always friendly when he entered our compound with a list of prisoners to transfer. He even began to query me regarding my well-being, which was unusual for a man like him who was known to thrive on doling out punishment. In his Detention Camp, recaptured escapees and thieves were held in deep pits so narrow the men had to sleep standing up.

Life began to settle into a routine. Normally I was busy inside the compound, and otherwise I hung out with our provost guards in the guard shack just outside the gate. The one-room structure had been fixed up over the months by adding partitions of wood and burlap and then plastering over the material with a sort of paste one of the painters had concocted from flour and other ingredients. For color, he filed shavings from bricks, crushed coal, brewed vegetables, and even requisitioned the yolks of a few eggs. He used the natural colors to paint beautiful murals on the burlap, which had been sized with the flour paste.

Our cooks had received special instructions from the provost guards on how to brew good English tea, and every morning at 10:00 a canister full of tea with sugar and milk added was delivered to the gatehouse. Around the same time a truck dropped off frosted buns, which the guards consumed with the tea. In due course I became a regular partaker of their hospitality, joining them almost every morning for those delectable snacks. We had become friends despite the more official wartime attitudes.

I was truly befuddled when one of the younger British gate guards asked me one day if I would like to come to town with him and a few of his mates one evening. He thought it would be a lot of fun and it would give me an opportunity to meet up with one of the Belgian girls. I didn't understand at first; I was young, unspoiled and a bit naive. Did I understand right, that he wanted me, a POW, to go to town with him and visit a nightclub? He was serious when he explained that I could accompany him to his billet and there change into one of his uniforms. He was convinced that I would not be questioned on account of any language flaw, for I spoke without an accent, though with a bit of a Yank slang perhaps.

He had discussed this with his mates and they were game. I, too, thought it could be a lot of fun; just the mere thought of it was a real joke.

I laughed, but I also knew the whole scheme was a bit too farfetched. I liked the idea and appreciated the invitation from the young Tommy, but the risk was much too great for me. To be caught impersonating a British soldier in a country that had learned to hate the Germans was scary, simply impossible. I begged off, but I felt good having been asked. It made me feel that young men, no matter what the color of their flag, can get along after all.

One day the Scottish sergeant came to the gate looking for me. "*Dolmetscher*, we have to conduct a search of prisoners that have been turned over to us by the Americans. How would you like to translate for me?" That sounded interesting; we had heard that the Americans were beginning to send their POWs back en masse. The sentinel to our compound passed me, saying, "Have fun, *Dolmetscher*," and we began to walk up the camp street. I was excited; it was the first time I had ventured out on the main camp thoroughfare.

The Scotsman and I walked past several of the other compounds before he pointed to the gate of a vacant enclosure. We headed in and joined a number of other British personnel who had arrived before us. The Main Lagerfuehrer, who had general administrative responsibility over all twenty compounds, was also there. A row of tables had been set up, and we took our positions. I stayed close to the Scotsman. A short time later a convoy of trucks pulled up near the gate and unloaded several hundred prisoners dressed in black uniforms with large white P.W. markings on the backs of their shirts and on their trousers. They were the POWs who were being repatriated from America, the first of many more to come. They all carried large duffel bags over their shoulders, some an extra bag in their free hand. They looked good, well fed and groomed, and well dressed, too: there were no mixed uniforms. They were cheerful on arrival, for they had been told they were going home.

Orders were passed to line up, to open their bags and empty the contents on the tables for inspection. My eyes popped when the first men emptied out their bags. There were cartons of cigarettes, bags of tobacco, new wallets, bars of chocolate and other candy, civilian neckties, toothbrushes and tubes of toothpaste—all things that were not available to us. I asked one of the men where he got all this from, how did he acquire it? He told me the POWs in America were paid for working and that they could buy the things we saw before us in their camp canteens. I couldn't deny feeling somewhat jealous and deprived.

The Main Lagerfuehrer, meanwhile, was consulting with some of the British officers, who were nodding their heads. He then proceeded to make a speech to the newly arrived men. After he welcomed them, he told them they had been very fortunate to have had the opportunity to acquire the goods and the mementoes they brought back with them. But, he stressed, there were 60,000 men at Camp 2228 who had not received a single cigarette in months. Some of these men had been selling their rings and watches for smokes; some were stuffing their pipes with black tea; still others were trading their food for cigarettes, exposing themselves to malnutrition. It would only be fair under the circumstances, the Lagerfuehrer went on, for the newcomers to share their wealth with those less fortunate men who had endured the transient facilities and poor conditions of 2228 for many months.

He made an impression on the men; they were nodding their heads as they conversed with others in the line. Then orders were passed to the searchers at the tables to confiscate all cigarettes except for two packs per man; similar instructions were given for the other items. Despite the Lagerfuehrer's speech, the frisking and the extent of the confiscation did not go over too well with the POW contingent from America. I had my hands full explaining the ruling again and again. Several objected to the treatment they were receiving. They had different ideas about things after having gone through *Umschulung*, a political reeducation course at Camp Eustis, Virginia. Reeducation? Did that make them any better than the poor suckers living in the mud of Camp 2228? Their complaints fell on deaf ears and the frisking continued.

Conditions were generally not good by late summer of 1945. The food, though meeting the prescribed calorie count, was at best just adequate. Some of the men with bad smoking habits parted with their rations for the satisfaction of a cigarette. It was primarily these men who suffered from malnutrition. Then there was an epidemic of dysentery. But despite prevailing conditions, camp morale received a boost when the "good things from America" taken from the repatriated prisoners were distributed. There were a few smiles here and there those days. The morale was kept at an acceptable level as more returnees from U.S. camps were brought in and additional confiscated items were distributed. Attitudes were given another boost in August 1945 when the prisoners were allowed to use International Red Cross mail to notify their families of their whereabouts.

In an effort to overcome the monotony of camp life, a theater group and a men's choir were formed in Compound 5. A large tent that could house fifty men was set aside as our recreation tent. Men dug the dirt out about a meter deep from the inside of one end of the tent; the undisturbed ground at the other end became the stage. The British supplied benches, which were set up for the spectators. Talented fellow prisoners tried their skills at light operettas with considerable success, while those with good voices formed a choir and arranged for recitals and also some sing-alongs, but without the rhythmic military tunes with which we all were most familiar.

Religious services were also offered in the big tent by a few ministers from among our POW contingent. Then there were the whittlers who carved chess figures, a game I learned while in Compound 5, and others who carved wooden cigarette cases with POW motifs on the sides. True pieces of artwork. And the teachers in our midst even volunteered their talents and services and started educational classes, including languages.

All these diversions, however, did not help those poor fellows who were faced with returning to areas of Germany occupied by the Russians. Everyone was afraid to return to their homes in the eastern parts of Germany, fearing they might never get there, but be deported enroute to perform reparations labor in the Soviet Union. We feared for the hundreds of Russians who were being lined up one day on the camp thoroughfare, getting ready to be shipped "home." These were fellows who had agreed to serve with the German forces after having been captured in the field. I recalled that we had about six of them assigned to our gun battery as ammunition handlers. They had been well-built and rugged, able to toss around our ammo cases with little effort. They, too, would be sent back to their home country, where they might not be welcomed. With what we knew of the Soviets and their system of political Kommissars, we doubted that many of them would ever see their families again.

In spite of the tensions, though, circumstances in the camp grew more relaxed for me. At noontime our gate guards locked the gates, leaving me alone in the guardhouse with the key while they went for lunch. Everything had become nonchalant. "If a working party comes back in the meantime, just let them in, *Dolmetscher,*" they'd say, or, "If a party has to leave while we are gone, let them out and give us the count when we get back." I was delighted to know they had learned to trust me.

During their absences I remained outside the gate holding the key to the large padlock tightly in my sweaty hands. I'd pass the time by talking with a German Luftwaffe noncom who was allowed to stay with me. He was building a model lighthouse with a beacon next to the road near the guard shed. He was thorough and worked slowly, carefully placing small pieces of granite in a bed of cement, layer after layer, taking pains to be sure his model would really look like a lighthouse. It did, and for several years remained one of a series of landmarks German POWs built along the main road leading through Camp 2228. It was our symbol, "the beacon in the night." Other compounds elected to build model churches, cathedrals, windmills and sandbox layouts of their section of the camp.

Most of the construction that went on in the camp was non-recreational, however. As fall approached, every effort was made to get ready for the cold weather, in case we would have to winter over in our tents. Shovels were signed out by the British and work details organized inside the compound, to dig out the earth from inside all the tents that housed any prisoners. The dirt was piled up around the tents as wind-breakers and excess dirt was carried in sacks to a central area in the rear of the compound and piled up. There were 250 or more tents in our compound by then and it took weeks of hard work to dig out the dirt. When this was finished, the dirt mound at the far end of our enclosure had become a small mountain, a nice place to stand and look about.

The British provided steel sheets for the floors of the tents and scrap wood with which to brace the sides to keep them from caving in. At that point, each man had been issued two blankets, and tinsmiths from within the compound began converting empty creosote drums into tent stoves and piping.

It seemed we were pretty well set for the winter, until the first heavy rain, when a number of the tents' pits filled up with water that had found its way through the burrows of field mice and other rodents. That was the fate of my tent—it was a disaster having to evacuate the flimsy shelter in the midst of a cloudburst. Later, when it turned colder and the tent stoves were lit, our misfortunes included a series of tent fires that wiped out what little the occupants had been able to call their own.

It was during the winter months of December 1945 and January 1946 that the first trainloads of German prisoners from Camp 2228 were repatriated to the Russian Zone of Germany. Among them were a few of my classmates who until then had been in Compound 5 with me. I was fortunate to be ordered to stay behind with the remaining members of our staff. We had to ready the camp to receive a new batch of incoming transient prisoners. As much as I wanted to return to my family, I didn't care for the rumors of being forced to work in the mines upon our return home. My school chums feared the worst; they were sullen when they finally departed.

Snow and winter weather often kept us in our tents for long periods of time. Life, even though of poor quality, had been more bearable earlier in the year. For a time, Compound 5 was empty, except for the remaining permanent staff. It was a time when we could rethink our lives and seek answers to our problems, each in his own way.

We quickly latched onto whatever bits and pieces of information became available on the progress of the war. Some of the most current news was obtained from our British captors. Though often dated, reports from new prisoners would help shed additional light on the data the British were passing on. All in all, there was little doubt that it would take a miracle to stop the onslaught of the Allies from the west and the Soviets from the east. Inwardly, we were hoping that the British and Americans would take the brunt of the Soviet attack. Whatever the outcome, the Russians had to be stopped, kept as far away as possible, out of Germany, away from our homes and families. In the waning days of the war, the prisoners were openly wishing for conflict between the Allies and the Russians. As haggard as most of us were, we were willing to throw in our lots with the Western powers to contribute our manpower and military skills in order to push the Mongolian hordes out of Germany and back to the Urals. We were there, doing nothing, just waiting and hoping. Perhaps it was too much to wish for.

We learned of the great strides British forces were making on their way to the Baltic Sea and in taking the German port cities of Hamburg, Bremen and Kiel. Timely as the information was, most of us captured near Minden hailed from central Germany, from towns and villages around the cities of Werdau and Schwarzenberg, both in Saxony. Therefore, we were primarily interested in what was going on in that sector, especially as the distance between the advancing Americans and the Soviets decreased from day to day. Forgetting what little our own forces could or might be doing to change the situation, I was rooting for the Amis to hurry along; to get there first, and even more so when the British told me that the First and Third U.S. Armies under Generals Hodges and Patton were virtually racing eastward on a line that would bring the men of one of these armies into our home towns and territory.

While the First Army made a dash for the Elbe River, meeting up with the Soviets at Torgau on 25 April, Patton's Third Army was moving rapidly eastward north of the Thueringer Wald, generally along the Autobahn in the direction Erfurt-Gera-Chemnitz. Following that route, the 76th Infantry Division took Crimmitschau, just eight kilometers north of Werdau, where our High School was. We had been drafted there the year before. The U.S. 89th Infantry Division was operating just below the 76th and approaching the city from the west through the Werdauer Wald, the forest where I had often played soldier and where we had bivouaced with the Hitler Youth from time to time.

I tried to concentrate on my work in Compound 5, but my heart was with my family at home in Fraureuth, a village stretched out along the country road between Greiz and Werdau. For a number of years we had rented a two-room upstairs apartment in a house on the Markt Platz which was on the main street through town. The building had been a brewery in years past. To our left, across a small dirt road, was the school I attended before transferring to the Oberschule in Werdau. Across the street from the school was the only hotel in town, the Rathskeller. Behind the school was the evangelical church, whose minister lived up a hill in a farmhouse that was visible from our front window, beyond the Markt Platz.

But now Dad and I were in the military, leaving Mother and my seven-year-old sister to fend for themselves during these crucial times. There was one consolation, however. Aunt Edith had returned from America soon after Germany declared war on the United States in December 1941. Her husband Werner, then employed by the German Consulate in New York, was expelled with other diplomats. Because she was a naturalized American citizen, Edith was given the choice of remaining in the United States or of accompanying her husband back to Germany. She was pregnant and elected to travel with her spouse. Following their arrival, they settled in Berlin, but after surviving many months of Allied bombings of the capital city, Edith finally sought refuge in our home, in the rural area of central Germany far from any military or economically important targets. She and her daughter Karin were still living with my family in the closing days of the war, and though the four of them had no choice but to share the crowded living space, there was a sense of togetherness in these times of distress, a feeling of security from each other's mere presence. Uncle Werner was working and stuck in Berlin. Being frozen in the job, he couldn't leave the devastated city and spent much of his time in air raid shelters praying to be spared from the hail of bombs that was tirelessly being dropped on the city.

It was as though a heavy burden had been lifted from my shoulders when I found out the Americans had occupied the area of my home town and were pushing onward in an easterly direction. My silent wish had come true. I knew my folks would do alright with the Americans, having lived among them before.

Besides, Edith was there and she was still a naturalized U.S. citizen.

But, suddenly and completely unexpectedly, word was spread in June that the Americans would be pulling out of central Germany and turning Saxony and Thuringia over to the Soviets. Impossible, I thought. The Americans wouldn't do a thing like that; to give up this large area in the heart of Germany to the Russians did not make any sense. This could be nothing more than an ugly rumor. But sure enough, I found out that the reports were true, and once more I started to fear for my family. My worries were based on rumors of brutal treatment of civilians by the Russians, sanctioned by their field commanders. The news articles and radio reports following the recapture by German forces of the town of Nemmersdorf in East Prussia in October 1944 had told of men, women and children being mercilessly annihilated. Also fueling my fears were my memories of the horrifying stories about Russian troop behavior that the refugees from the eastern parts of Germany had told us on their westward trek through our villages in central Germany. These people had fled the approaching Soviet forces on foot and by horse and wagon a few short months before, just to keep ahead and out of the way of the Russians.

Only our neighbors with known communistic leanings—and there were a number of them—would hail the Soviet takeover. They had kept a low profile during the war, but they were known. They were the ones who never had anything good to say about Germany's successes and early victories. They were the complainers, people who were just waiting for the National Socialists to be plowed under. Fraureuth had been a Communist stronghold long before Hitler took over the reins of government in January 1933. Fanatics in our town had raised the red flag with the hammer and sickle on the highest chimney of the porcelain factory on 1 May 1933, a full three months after the Nazis took control. Their time might now have come again.

For all of us the Third Reich and Grossdeutschland were things of the past. To me and my comrades from the Werdau region as well as our families, the American presence in our villages and towns would soon also be no more than a memory of a time when new beginnings could have been in the offing. With the Russians in our homes, all we could think of was being condemned and doomed to living our lives behind a solid wall of Soviet bayonets.

4

Childhood

Mom and Dad were among the many Germans who migrated to the United States in the 1920s in hopes of finding a new and better life following Germany's defeat in the first World War. Individually, they had joined the droves of eager Germans that flocked to the United States, proclaimed as the land of milk and honey. They met, were married, and settled down in the city of Pawtucket, Rhode Island, a year or so before I was born in 1928.

We moved to New York before I was five. My folks managed a rooming house on 18th Street in Manhattan, a venture that lasted but a few years. Living in the basement apartment had not been appealing, and the unwanted excitement that went with the job was sufficiently discouraging to prompt my parents to look for ways to get out. Once the police came in with drawn guns to flush out a group of gangsters who had holed up in one of the apartments. Then there had been reports that a Chinese spy was living just upstairs from us. All this was very exciting to me, but too dangerous and upsetting to my folks. Dad's health was not the best at the time, and even I was termed a *Kellerpflanze* (a cellar plant) by our German doctor, who felt I was in need of fresh air and sun. Our surroundings were far from ideal. I played in a little fenced-in yard in the rear of our five-story tenement house in lower Manhattan, a dreary place, painting faces on the boards with crayon to make it look happy like a circus.

We frequented stores in Yorkville that sold German-made products, among them imported toy soldiers, which I collected. For Christmas in 1935, Dad set up my train in the living room of our flat with all the perfectly scaled soldiers I owned. It was an impressive display, complete with houses, an airport, a forest, a castle and even a reviewing stand with miniatures of Hitler, Goering and other leaders of the Third Reich. On the wall to the rear of the display was the *Reichskriegsflagge,* Germany's new battle flag. My folks liked the layout so much they called in a professional photographer to take a picture, but only after Dad had replaced the German banner with the flag of the United States.

I liked playing with my soldiers; I wanted to be one myself one day when I grew up. I'd play soldier whenever I could. One evening in New York when my folks had company, I came in from the next room to ask Dad if I could use his grey felt hat for a helmet. He said yes. After I cut the brim off and trimmed the sides to make it look more like a real German helmet I paraded through the living-room. Dad was speechless, completely dumb-founded. I had cut up his best hat, the one he wore with his suit. He managed to keep his composure, and everyone laughed. Lucky for me there were no repercussions, even after the company had left.

Playing with the neighbors' kids was also great fun. We often played with marbles on the serrated sewer cover near where we later lived on East 90th Street in New York. I often ventured with my friend Paul, who lived two houses away, into the darkness of his cellar with flashlights on pretend search missions, especially when there had been a break-in, kidnapping or other more hair-raising situation in the neighborhood. Scared though we were, we always sought out adventures, sometimes without comprehending the risks we were taking.

Then there was Charlie, the kid next door. His older brother was a whiz at making airplane models from balsa wood kits. He had many of the painted miniatures hanging from their living-room ceiling, and I often wished I owned one of them. Years later, as I scanned the Allied bomber formations flying overhead on their missions of destruction, I would often wonder if Paul or Charlie or his older brother were up there with them while I was on the ground wishing for the planes to fall from the sky.

In the heat of the New York summer we sometimes put a barrel over the fire hydrant on our street and then turned on the water. What fun to get soaked, fully dressed, under the stream of water that first shot upwards and then dropped down on us like a waterfall, a cool and refreshing gift from heaven. When the cops came, we all ran for it. Once around the corner we'd stop at the drug store for one of those delicious Mello Rolls of french vanilla ice cream, the likes of which I never tasted in Germany. If we didn't have any money we might just swipe an apple from an open box outside the corner grocery store.

I also have fond memories of the funnies in the Sunday papers. The Katzenjammer Kids were my favorites, maybe because of their funny accents, but I was also a fan of Tiny Tim and Little Orphan Annie. I loved listening to the latest episodes being read over the radio or by Mom when she'd read them to me. The funnies were unique to America.

Then there were the warm, freshly baked buns Dad would bring home from the bakery just in time for breakfast on Sundays. What a treat. With a cold glass of fresh homogenized milk the morning fare had always been fit for a king. I never could stand drinking milk in Germany. Though it was delivered fresh and foamy, direct from the cow the way I liked it, Grandma Adam had decreed that the milk would be boiled before drinking. I hated it that way, especially the skin that formed on the top. It gave me an upset stomach just looking at it. And if I did chance a drink and got a glob of it in my mouth I would choke on it and throw up for sure.

Dad had worked for Ruppert's Brewery just around the corner, but to keep financially afloat, he also was a ticket taker in a nearby moviehouse that showed German films. Every now and then he asked Mom and me to join him at the theater to see one of the newly arrived feature presentations. I was always anxious to go when a new military film had come in. I remember seeing *Kreuzer Emden* with Marlene Dietrich singing in her deep voice. But the film that left the deepest impression on me was a World War I feature entitled *Stosstrupp 1917*, Combat Patrol 1917. The scene that stuck in my mind over the years was the sight of a wounded English or American soldier lying in a dugout surrounded by Germans, calling for his mother in painful agony. Years later, fate would have it that I witnessed a similar scene, a severely wounded British soldier lying in a ditch, calling for his mother. I would always wonder if he survived his ordeal.

My first trip to Germany was in 1934 when I was six years old. My Mom and I visited her family that summer for a full three months. Her relatives lived in a small town in Saxony, in central Germany where there were lots of open fields, fresh air and plenty of sunshine, everything as prescribed for me by the doctor. It was just a year after Hitler had become Reichs Chancellor. We witnessed several parades while there. Oh, how I loved the marching formations, the sounds of the fife and drum corps, the rhythm of the cadence being beat out by the drums, and the perfect marching order of the columns of uniformed men and youths. I knew already that I would become a soldier some day. Though I was much too young to join the youth movement, my relatives nevertheless outfitted me with a complete Hitler Youth uniform. I wore and showed off my outfit with pride even if I couldn't march along with the others. Uncle Erich, a *Pfadfinder* (much like the Boy Scouts, until Hitler's takeover), had joined the Youth Movement in its early days and was making great strides on his way up the leadership ladder.

When we returned to America after that beautiful vacation, I had forgotten how to speak English. In a week or so, however, I was again able to converse with the kids on my street. After coming back we seemed to be spending more time on 86th Street where the New York Germans congregated. Whenever we went there, we visited one of the cafeterias and had the rich, creamy German torte, or the thin-layered butter cream cakes. My mother found great delight in these fancy German pastries and also in the variety of milk chocolates available. To us it was just like Germany. Cafe Geiger was one of her favorite stops when we went shopping. And right up the street from there, just across Third Avenue, was the Automat. What a place! There were walls of prepared foods in small glass compartments, everything from sandwiches and fruit salads to cakes and pies. All we had to do to make our selection was to insert a few coins, open the door, take out the goodies and sit down to eat at one of the tables. Not too far from there was a place that sold tropical drinks. I stopped there frequently with my father, too.

My Dad felt so proud in the changes taking place in Germany and in the way the Fatherland had bounced back after World War I and the great inflation, that he decided to join the German *Bund* in New York. He looked sharp when he went to their meetings, all dressed up in his uniform. People looked and stretched their necks as he walked down the street on his way to the Third Avenue elevator. His shiny black boots and riding breeches fit him perfectly, as did his white shirt with the black, white and red armband with the swastika in the center. We visited a camp the organization ran in Long Island one day. There was a parade with massed German banners, just like I had seen in Germany, except here, the Stars and Stripes was among them. It felt good seeing the two flags that had become meaningful to me flying side by side. Yet Dad at times spoke of hecklers who tried to crash their assemblies at Madison Square Garden, which I couldn't comprehend at the time.

What a great day it had been when Germany's newest dirigible, the LZ-129 *Hindenburg*, flew over New York on its way to Lakehurst. Standing in the street below, we cheered at the sight of this flying marvel with the swastikas painted on its fins. Dad quickly befriended some of the officers and crew and one day he and I were invited to board the zeppelin for a visit while it was at anchor. I felt so proud to tour the dirigible with my Dad.

I understood why he was shocked and disappointed at the news of the fire and explosion that destroyed the *Hindenburg*, just as the zeppelin was coming in for another landing. Germany's pride, the symbol of the Reich's early achievements and progress, had gone up in flames and smoke. A number of his friends had been badly burned in the disaster. I remember visiting them in a New York hospital and seeing their bandaged heads and arms, no faces, just bandages, all pitiful sights. Dad said that it could have been avoided had the United States made some of its helium gas available for the zeppelin project. Due to the lack of helium, the

Germans had had no alternative but to use combustible gas to keep the dirigible airborne—which resulted in disaster.

The big change in our lives was beginning to take shape when I was permitted to accompany my aunt Edith on a trip to Germany in the summer of 1937. I was nine years old then. I just couldn't leave home without packing a box of my German toy soldiers to take along. Everywhere we went after our arrival, whether to visit my aunt's grandmother in Magdeburg or my mother's family in Saxony, I was always quick to set up a battle group in the dirt or grass the first chance I had.

On this trip I was again presented with a Hitler Youth uniform by my German relatives. During this stay I was also invited to accompany my cousin Erhard when he attended his mandatory weekly meetings for youths ten years and older. It sounded like fun, so I put on my uniform and tagged along. My cousin introduced me to the group leader of *Faehnlein* 39/133, the Youth group of the town of Leubnitz, and I was told to line up with the rest of the boys. There were strange commands I had never heard before, so I did as the others did. Soon we marched out of the school yard—I was quick to pick up the marching step—and headed up a small alley and out of the village onto open farmland.

Orders were passed to take advantage of any natural camouflage. I observed the boys breaking branches from trees and shrubs and holding them in front of their bodies as they hiked past some dense growth at the edge of a small wooded area. I followed suit and hid my face behind the leaves of a branch while we were walking along. We turned down a narrow path running through open fields. After hiking for a distance I suddenly received a slap on my back from one of the youth leaders. He was yelling his head off about how stupid I was for carrying my camouflage tree out into the open where it stood out like a sore thumb. Erhard came to my rescue by telling him I was only visiting from America. The young leader was quick to apologize, but took the time to give me my first lecture, a five-minute private lesson, on proper camouflage procedures. I never made the same mistake again. He knew what he was talking about, for many others told me the same things in later years.

I attended German school while we were visiting. It was not

easy, even though I had been taking private lessons in Yorkville for over a year before going on the trip. I had learned to write German script pretty well and spoke the language fluently; we had spoken it at home. But their way of calculating mathematical problems was another story. It was much different from the way I had learned in the New York Public School System. Of necessity I spoke German, did my thinking in English and performed my calculations the American way, the way I had learned.

The most difficult and discouraging thing, however, was trying to keep up with the German kids in athletics and gym classes. They climbed poles and ropes like monkeys, up and down seemingly without effort. Vigorous training at school and in the Hitler Youth had paid off well. They were truly as Hitler wanted them to be: "Hart wie Kruppstahl, zaeh wie Leder und flink wie die Windhunde," hard as Krupp steel, tough as leather and fast as greyhounds. The lack of prior athletic training was to my disadvantage to the point that I was mocked and ridiculed by Herr Heidrich—a grouchy tobacco-chewing teacher—for having pudding under my skin instead of muscles.

At P.S. 151 in New York we had played tag, run relay races and things of that sort—nothing comparable with the level of physical conditioning going on in the German schools. In America we also never wore gym clothes, but did our exercises in street clothing. In Germany the kids wore gym suits or uniforms, black shorts with white sleeveless tops. They were exceptionally well disciplined and knew how to follow orders. Even though I had begun to dislike some of them for their snide remarks about me being an American weakling, I did admire their athletic performance and the skills they displayed on the various types of gym equipment, the horse, the rings, the parallel bars, the trampoline. They were in good shape, something I could not say of myself at that time. It was at times like this that I would get homesick for my Mom and Dad, and for America.

It had been planned that Aunt Edith and I would return home to America after a stay of two months or so in Germany. The time to get ready for the journey was nearing and I was looking forward to the trip back to New York, to Cracker Jacks, popcorn, backed beans, ketchup, Jello, bananas, all the things we couldn't get in

Germany. Instead, Mother joined us in what was supposed to be another visit to her family. Aunt Edith returned to America alone. After another enjoyable month or so of visits and family get-togethers it was finally time to pack for the trip home.

On the way to the railroad station in Werdau to make travel arrangements, we were stopped by a mailman on a bicycle who handed a telegram to my mother. She looked surprised; it was from Dad in New York, and read: "Stay. Have found work in Germany. Coming."

We were happy at the mere thought of Dad joining us so we could be a family again. But despite that momentary joy there were many questions that had to be answered regarding his plans for our future.

Our apprehension was lifted when Dad arrived late in 1937 and told us he had found work at the *Arbeitsamt,* the Labor Office, of the city of Crimmitschau, about twelve kilometers from where we had been offered temporary shelter in Oma Adam's two-room apartment. That he was able to latch on to a government job so close to where Mother really wanted to stay was a miracle; Dad felt moving to Germany was the right thing to do. There was no turning back now anyway; before leaving New York he had given up our apartment on 90th Street and sold the furniture and the household items they had accumulated over the years. Now we would have to remain in Germany, like it or not, and make the best of it. Mother was content to settle near her sister Frieda, who also lived in Leubnitz and within walking distance of their mother.

Two immediate problems were to find a place to live, and to locate a store that would accept us as a customer and supply us with a weekly allocation of butter, which was in scarce supply. Living arrangements were the first order of business. Housing was scarce and there were long waiting lists for the growing number of workers' families, some with priority entitlements, or party pull. Dad marched to the *Gemeindeamt,* the local town hall, but without any luck. Checking with local party officials did not produce any help or hope for the immediate future; only so many buildings were approved for construction and it would be quite a while before housing units would be available.

For the immediate future there was no alternative but to stay with Oma Adam on a semi-permanent basis. She was lucky to have been assigned an apartment in one of the new six-apartment brick houses the government built in the *Arbeiter Siedlung,* the workers' settlement. She was doing well, receiving her old age pension plus a variety of other aid, including free periodic food allocations via the community-wide *Pfundsammlungen,* collections of one-pound food donations from workers and their families, who were expected by the party to make such contributions for the benefit of the elderly. The three of us moved in with her, and though she readily agreed, living space was cramped. Now I understand what was meant when they said "Germany needs more space for its people."

Oma gave up her bedroom to my folks and I slept in a neighbor's apartment. Oma lived in the combination living room kitchen, sleeping on her couch at night. The coal stove was in her room, as well as the only sink in the apartment, so all washing, including dishes, had to be done in the one room that was hers under this awkward arrangement. Our toilet, working on the gravity principle, and without water, was halfway down the front stairs in the entry hall. It served the three families on the upper floor, including the four of us. A farmer using a handpump emptied the cesspool from time to time, which seemed a neverending process. We were always glad when he left our yard in his horse-drawn honey wagon on the way to the nearby fields to fertilize his crops.

The land around each building was divided up among the tenants, who used every inch of the area to plant vegetables, and a few flowers, space permitting. At the cellar level there was a wash kitchen with a large coal-fired cauldron to boil the water and clothes. Large wooden wash buckets were available for community use along with a hand operated wringer and a mangle for pressing sheets. We enjoyed taking a bath down there once a week in the portable metal tub Oma kept in her cellar.

That winter, Oma allowed me to take out the old wooden sled that had belonged to uncle Erich. She had stored and kept it as a keepsake. I roughed it that day, and as I was flying over a low compacted mound of snow meant for skiers, I broke off the left runner of the sled. She was furious and unforgiving when I brought the remains home. It was the first time I realized she had a temper. I felt saddened at the mishap, and tried to point out the many tiny holes all over the sled that could have contributed to weakening the wood, but she wouldn't have any part of it. She mumbled about my coming from America and breaking things on her.

The workers' settlement was a complex of fifty or more multifamily houses, the first having been built soon after Hitler came to power in 1933. More were being added each year. For the convenience of the people in the *Siedlung* situated within a ten-minute walk from the main village of Leubnitz, there were several shops: a bakery, grocery store, butcher and even a shoemaker. In the center of the settlement was a large *Sportplatz* and on the far side of the field, a spanking new youth hostel. The entire area was a showplace, everything new, neat, clean and well kept.

With our housing arrangements taken care of—at least temporarily—Dad turned his attention to the matter of food supplies. Becoming aligned with a grocer who would accept us as a customer was a difficult task, simply because the stores were allotted only a limited quantity of the merchandise in short supply, with no apparent leeway for upward adjustments. Therefore, most incoming shipments of scarce food supplies were earmarked and reserved for the registered customers. There was just no way we could share in such merchandise until someone moved or died, or unless the commodities became more plentiful. This matter turned into a mad task for Dad. He had a hard time with it, in particular with the butter. For a limited period the store in the *Siedlung* was able to accommodate us, but gave notice early on that we would have to find another outlet.

Luckily, Dad was given a tip to check with a store in Fraureuth, the next village just across the fields. Herr Seidel, the store proprietor, was very accommodating and signed us on as permanent customers, assuring us of our entitlements to the controlled commodities. The drawback was that we would have to hike two or three kilometers each way to do our shopping. So long as the weather was warm, this was a pleasant walk; sometimes we took the little wooden wheeled hand wagon to lighten the burden of carrying the bundles. The winter months proved more difficult, however. For those necessary weekly trips I would strap on skis and a knapsack, and brave the icy winds howling across the flat, open fields. When my ears and toes started to thaw out and itch like crazy after I returned and warmed up in front of the hot stove, I wished there were an easier way to get our food supplies. Those journeys could be torturous at times.

I also made trips to the baker for Oma; since we didn't have an adequate oven, cakes had to be brought to the baker to be cooked. Oma Adam periodically rolled out the dough for four or five large flat round cakes and covered them with fruit, chocolate or streussel before I carted them to the baker on her small hand wagon. The challenge not to pick the fruit or streussels from the warm cakes after they came out of the oven tested my self control. There was no need to sneak a taste though. Oma always rewarded me with a great big piece from any cake of my choice; I'd pick plums most of the time. There was coffee and cake every afternoon, and when she ran out of Kuchen, she'd make a new batch for me to take to the baker.

In early 1938 our neighbors' daughter, a girl about five years older than I, asked one day, "When is your mother going to have her baby?"

I didn't know what to say; she had to be fooling. "What do you mean?"

"Well, haven't you noticed how fat your mother has been getting?"

"No, and if she were, so what?"

"Don't you know when women get a fat belly, they have babies?"

I stared in disbelief, "No, they don't." I didn't know what she was talking about.

"Oh, you don't know anything," she said, "Come, let me tell you about it."

I was upset, but I was curious, so I listened. My mother had been putting on weight, but she liked and ate lots of German milk chocolates, pralines, and all kinds of cakes and torte. That would make her fat. After my talk with the neighbor girl, however, a seed of curiosity had been planted and I snuck a look at Mother the first chance I got. Gosh, she did have a really fat belly and she looked different than some of the other fat women in the neighborhood.

March 13 was a day of great excitement. My folks had company the very first thing in the morning. I was first sent off to the baker for some fresh rolls. When I got up the stairs, Dad took them from me and then had me wait in front of the house on the street for the milk lady to come by for a liter of fresh milk. She took forever to come around the corner. I was getting impatient, and I was hungry. This time, Dad greeted me at the door. He was all smiles: "You always wanted a little sister, and now the stork brought one for you."

I was dumbfounded, but had an embarrassed smile on my face; I felt it turning red. Why did he say I always wanted a little sister? I never said anything like that, and of all things, a sister. . . ? And now he was saying the stork brought her. I was confused. Ma was in bed smiling and holding a little bundle all wrapped up in a blanket. Why was she in bed if the stork brought the baby? I didn't ask, I just kissed my mother and gave Sister a quick peek; I had to get out of there. This was quite a surprise, a little too much first thing in the morning. I needed time to think. I wanted to do something. It was time to eat anyway, so I went to the next room where Oma was. She gave me a nice crispy roll with butter and a cup of cocoa.

We turned on the *Volksempfaenger,* Oma's small people's radio, the kind every family had. There was marching music, just what I liked, with all that rhythm. I could envision columns of troops parading in some big city, proudly goose-stepping past the reviewing stand, "eyes right," in honor of some dignitary. An announcer broke in to give a report on Germany's annexation of Austria. What? There had been reports of tensions in Austria and I thought I remembered hearing of an ultimatum being issued either by the Schuschnigg government in Vienna, or from Germany. Either way, this seemed to be it. The papers were full of pictures of the orderly takeover by the Wehrmacht that day. Der Fuehrer had been quick to come to the aid of his countrymen when Schuschnigg stepped down on the urging of his own people. Hitler made it a point to make a triumphant entry into Braunau, the place of his birth; he had been an Austrian. Now there would be no difference, all the German-speaking people would be united in a single country.

"Ein Volk, ein Reich, ein Fuehrer," became the epic slogan of the times. Everything had gone smoothly, there no longer was an Austria, now there just was a Grossdeutschland, a Greater Germany. However, the will of the people should be tested. In early April a plebiscite was held giving the people an opportunity to say yes or no. The Austrian vote was almost unanimous in favor of the annexation. Even we kids in Germany were required to vote in school. I was fascinated by all the excitement, the flag-waving, the marching music, the greatness of Germany and of the times, and I knew how I would vote.

When it was over and the count had been taken, Herr Heidrich, our teacher, stood before the class with his arms crossed, chewing tobacco as always. He was scanning up and down the aisles of desks with penetrating and probing eyes; he seemed angry. He seemed to be looking for someone, searching for something. Then he took a deep breath and said, "There is one among you who dared vote no: who is it?" His voice got louder as he spoke. Everyone froze, total silence, not a word was uttered. Who would have been so silly as to vote no? Maybe someone's parents had been talking against the Fuehrer's actions at home. If so, they should be made to answer. The silence continued, then, "Schröder, you're from America, I bet you voted no."

Everyone turned toward me, staring, some with hate in their eyes, others mumbling to one another. I was scared. "No, Herr Heidrich I was not the one." He continued his tirade, threatening to wallop the one who did it with his bamboo stick, when he found him out. That close call upset me for the rest of the day. I had done no wrong; I was offended and felt like hiding somewhere. Even after school, the kids kept nagging me, asking if I was the one who prevented our class from getting a 100 percent yes vote. I knew there were several in our class who couldn't read without difficulty; perhaps they should be asking them if they understood the ballot. I felt alone, deserted, even in the company of my schoolmates, as we headed home.

We were playing soldiers a lot those days and found a perfect spot in a clay quarry facing Werdau, the city adjoining the village of Leubnitz. First we would lay out fortifications along the upper rim of the steep cliffs, and then dig earthworks, trenches with machine gun nests, observation points, everything we could think of that might be built into real defensive works like the West Wall facing France which had been initiated about that time. Most of my friends were Protestants. Our positions were facing an area of Werdau inhabited by Catholics, and for the most part, they were private homeowners, *Eigenheimer* as we called them. Whether it was jealousy because of their wealth, or resentment of their religion, no one knew; they were just the enemy and we would carry out our make-believe bombardments whenever we had a chance to play at war. We always won.

I turned ten at the end of March and my time had come to officially enroll in the Jungvolk, the Hitler Youth organization for ten- to fourteen-year-olds. I had already unofficially participated in some of their meetings and drills, to get to know them and to further my germanization process. Enrollment was mandatory under an edict of 1936 which required all German youths to be raised physically, intellectually and morally to serve the people and society. And so, with great ceremony, as a band played and we raised high our black flags with the sign of lightning, a number of us were sworn in to *Faehnlein* 39/133, to "do our duties at all times in love and faithfulness to the Fuehrer and the flag, so help us God."

We were drilled rigorously, preparing for the *Pimpfenprobe*, a series of achievement tests which would determine whether we met the government's physical and mental standards for children our age. There was much to learn: the history of Hitler's rise to power including his personal biography, a series of Hitler Youth and military songs, close order drill, camouflage principles, map and compass reading. Then came a series of physical exercises that had to be accomplished, including running, jumping, swimming, and ball as well as hand grenade throwing. Satisfactory completion of all the requirements and tests entitled us to wear a *Fahrtenmesser*, a camping knife, on the belt of our uniform. It was an outward sign of our accomplishment. The blade of the dagger was inscribed: "Blut und Ehre," blood and honor. We wore it with pride and liked to show it off. From this time on, we were expected to abide by the motto of the Jungvolk: "We are hard, silent and loyal; we are comrades, and we uphold our honor to the highest."

Later in the summer an armored unit of the Wehrmacht came to Leubnitz for maneuvers. This was a grand time for us boys. The light tanks were lined up in a long row near the railroad bridge, along the little creek that ran the length of the village. We were dying to climb on top of one of these steel monsters and look it over. We had seen pictures of tanks in the papers when our troops had moved into Austria a few months earlier, but we had never seen a real one. This was our chance. We asked the guard, and to our amazement, he let us climb on one of the tanks and crawl around on it. But all too soon he told us to get off and to be on our way. We didn't want to go; the tanks were great. If only we were a little older so we could drive one of them. One day maybe we would, but for now we had to be satisfied just to play.

Several of us decided to do just that; we pretended to be the enemy and hatched a plan to sneak up on the guard, jump him, and then scramble to the top of a tank as a sign of our victory. We slowly made our way up the line of parked tanks and then, without the guard noticing, skirted between two of them. Then we headed back toward the guard, moving along on the far side, behind the tanks. When we drew close enough, we crossed back to the side where we had last seen the sentinel. There he was! I was closest; a mad dash from behind and I was on his back with my arms around him. He twisted and turned, and shook me off quickly, unslinging his rifle in the process. In the meantime the others were scrambling to the top of the nearest tank. The guard cussed and yelled, calling us all "damned dogs" while he chased us down the line of tanks he was watching. We made a turn for an alley and kept running. We were scared; we shouldn't have done what we did, but the temptation to play partisan was too great. We were lucky the sentinel didn't take aim and shoot; we were too close for him to miss. We felt sick to our stomachs as we made our way back to the *Siedlung*.

There was talk of unrest among the Germans in the *Sudetenland*, and that the Czechs were persecuting them. Soon after, groups of refugees from that area came to town with just a few bundles of personal belongings, mostly women and children, some pulling their small wooden hand wagons in which they had piled the meager possessions they were able to take when they left their homes. They were given temporary shelter at Gasthof Heil near the Werdau city line. We were told they had to flee in a hurry, or risk being killed. We all felt bad for these poor people. Something ought to be done about the situation; the Czechs just couldn't be allowed to get away with this. The *Sudetenland Freikorps* was formed about that time, to come to the aid of our brothers and sisters across the border. Members of the Korps would cross the frontier at night, avoiding contact with Czech patrols, and escort back into the Reich those Germans who were willing to chance the illegal crossing under the guns of the border guards. By the end of September, the situation had mushroomed to international proportions, resulting in the signing of the Munich Agreement by Germany, Italy, England and France, which compelled the Czechs to cede the *Sudetenland* to Germany.

As the summer passed, Dad was often out looking for a place of our own. Oma had been a great supporter of our family in the early days but after all this time, she was beginning to feel the loss of her privacy; the nightly crying of my baby sister didn't help. One day Dad announced we would be moving to Fraureuth, the town where we had been buying our food for the past few months. It was there that he came across a married couple willing to share their four-room flat in a section of the old porcelain factory that had been converted to apartments. Although Mother once again had to share a kitchen with another family, we were fortunate to have a well-furnished living and sleeping area for ourselves, and the knowledge that we were not infringing on the privacy of the host. The apartment was well kept. It was a pleasure living there. Out in front of the building, in the center of the old factory complex, was an area of greens with a fountain and benches where Mother would often sit with my sister Annerose in her lap.

In March the following year, there was more military action. The Wehrmacht took over large areas of what was left of Czechoslovakia. Bohemia and Moravia were occupied and became a protectorate of the Reich. The remaining section, Slovakia, seized Hitler's offer to declare its independence, but remained under the protective umbrella of Germany, instead of running the risk of also being occupied. A week later, on 23 March, Hitler laid claim to the city of Memel, located near the frontier of East Prussia, just over the border and in Lithuania. Everyone seemed enthusiastically in favor of the Fuehrer's actions to bring into the fold all areas with a sizeable German population.

Having moved to a new town required my formal transfer to the rolls of *Faehnlein* 12/96 of the Jungvolk organization in Fraureuth. In July, our group embarked on a one-week march and cross-country hike through Thuringia, to attend the National Hitler Youth Encampment at Rudolstadt, which was booked as "Die Leistungsschau der HJ," the achievement show of the Hitler Youth. This took a lot of preparation; during our mandatory weekly meetings on Tuesday evenings and Saturday afternoons we were busy building a two-wheeled baggage cart with bicycle wheels and rubber tires. Packing our heavy backpacks into the cart would make our hike much easier, even though it would take six of us to push and pull the cart all the way to camp. We knew it wouldn't be easy, but it appeared more reasonable than having to carry the packs on our backs all the time. Besides, we would be able to rotate between the cart detail and less strenuous tasks such as cooking, hauling firewood and water, etc.

The distance to Rudolstadt was some eighty kilometers, with the planned route taking us into the foothills of the Thueringer Wald, where we would be carting our wagon up and down the hilly terrain. The project was a tremendous challenge for us. We made it, overcoming daily hardships and patching several flat tires along the way. From time to time the fully loaded cart became too heavy to move, and our leaders—who were from the senior Hitler Youth, ranging in age from fifteen to eighteen—helped carry some of our backpacks in addition to their own. We of the Jungvolk admired these fellows for their physical fitness and willingness to give us a hand. We felt we were among comrades and didn't feel intimidated just because we were younger.

Along our route we slept in barns, or in tents we pitched in the woods. Oh, how good it felt to drop into the hay for a good night's sleep, after a long day's hike in hot weather. We learned what sweating meant and how to cope with blistering feet. A jump in a creek or river was the refreshing treat we longed for after pushing the cart for a prolonged period of time.

As soon as we arrived in Rudolstadt, we were quickly directed to an assembly point where we were integrated into marching units with thousands of other youths who had come from all over central Germany. We were tired and worn out, but we all quickly perked up when we were told to line up ten abreast to parade past the Youth Leader of the Reich. We brushed off our uniforms; wiped the dust from our shoes; combed our hair; straightened out our uniforms, making sure our shirts were tucked into our pants properly; and did everything we could to look sharp. We were proud to be here to participate in the pass and review before Baldur von Schirach, our Reichsjugendfuehrer, whom none of us had ever seen before in person. Then we were off, marching down the streets of Rudolstadt. The people of the city turned out in droves to make us feel welcome. The deep, low-pitched thumping of drums ahead of us beat out the cadence for us to follow, boom, boom, boom-boom-boom. We soon got in step; the sound of massed fanfares quickly brought us to attention. We were nearing the reviewing stand. "Achtung, Augen rechts," attention, eyes right, and we were passing at attention right in front of our leader. For us, this was a great moment.

Immediately following the review, the Reichsjugendfuehrer addressed the thousands who were now assembled, all neatly aligned and in formation, on a large open meadow surrounded by hundreds of round and square squad tents. He told us that England had begun to call up children for military service, but Germany had no need to, words that gave us reassurance that we had a strong and powerful army that could defend the Fatherland against any external aggression. We knew, though, that it was our duty and responsibility to do our best in anything we undertook; we, too, would be doing our share for the betterment of Germany.

After being assigned to our tents in the vast city of canvas, we marched to the field kitchens to receive our first meal in camp. We were amazed at the huge size of the field kitchens; they must have had three or four large cauldrons mounted in a row on a special trailer built to feed masses of people. There were two such trailers in use and the cooking staff consisted of Wehrmacht personnel. It

Stars, Stripes and Swastikas set the tone for
my 1935 Christmas display in New York.
(*Author's collection*)

Showing off my brand new
Hitler Youth uniform during
my visit to Germany in 1934
when I was six years old.
(*Author's collection*)

All looked well in 1936 when Stars and
Stripes and Swastikas flew side by side at a
parade of the German *Bund* in Long
Island. (*Author's collection*)

Learning to take a rifle apart and reassemble it speedily gave us a feeling of accomplishment. (*Bundesarchiv, Koblenz, Germany*)

The Jungvolk Fanfarenzug was always up front when our Youth group marched through town. (*Bibliothek fuer Zeitgeschichte, Stuttgart, Germany*)

We hiked for days on end to participate at one of the mass Youth encampments where we could show off our skills. (*Bibliothek fuer Zeitgeschichte, Stuttgart, Germany*)

In December 1944 we received our silver epaulet stripes making us Luftwaffenoberhelfer. Now we were sixteen-year-old auxiliarists, but there were no subordinates. (*Author's collection*)

88mm antiaircraft guns in firing position waiting for the enemy bomber formations that were sure to come. (*Bundesarchiv, Koblenz, Germany*)

Regular flak member flanked by L H Leithold (left) and me, standing in front of our range finder. (*Eberhard Leithold, Germany*)

A quick pose during an alert. The two soldiers to my left are wearing Flak Activity Badges on their left sleeves. The rings painted on the range finder, at right, show that our battery had been credited with downing five enemy bombers. (*Author's collection*)

was just fantastic that everything had been arranged so well, all for the Hitler Youth. In the evening we built a camp fire in our assigned tent area and sang stirring youth and marching songs we all knew by heart. We had learned all of the rousing melodies as part of our early training.

In the days that followed we were constantly drilled in close order formations, lectured in political philosophy, and subjected to the most rigorous physical training ever, requiring total commitment and exertion. We ran, jumped, climbed, double-timed, crawled and rolled in the dirt, then started all over again, adding push-ups, rope pulling and other exercises that left us completely exhausted by day's end. Many a tear was shed during those two weeks and though we may have felt sorry for ourselves and wished we had not come, when it was over we had forgotten the torment. We had been whipped into shape and, oh, how good we now felt; we were proud, we were important. The encampment had truly been a show of accomplishments. Because we had done so well, we were granted the bonus of being permitted to take the train home, rather than repeating the strenuous eighty-kilometer hike up and down the hilly terrain.

Soon after we returned home, in early August, an entire division of troops was routed through our town coming from the direction of Greiz. They were heading east for fall maneuvers, we were told. The procession lasted for two days and nights, without letup: tanks, scout cars, trucks with supplies, infantry units, entire sections on bicycles, a constant flow of men and equipment. Never in our lives had we seen so many troops in one place at one time. We wondered if they were really going on maneuvers, or if they were heading for the Polish border. No one actually knew, but the situation with Poland did not look good. Hitler had asked for the return of the free city of Danzig and a road through the Polish corridor, linking the Reich with East Prussia, but chances of getting his way without the use of force were not too promising. Instead, the Poles were going after the German civilians living in the corridor area; reports of horror and death filled the newspapers.

The sudden signing of a nonaggression pact between Germany and the Soviet Union on 23 August came as an unexpected surprise. The Communists and the Nazis had been arch-enemies in the days of Hitler's rise to power; there had never been anything these two countries had in common, so the news of the treaty came as a shock to many, including our family. We were baffled. The Communist functionaries in Germany had been rounded up and thrown into concentration camps, and now this treaty? It didn't take very long for rumors to surface that it no longer made any difference if we greeted each other with "Heil Moscow," instead of "Heil Hitler." To top it off, a number of Communists in our area were released from imprisonment and sent home as a gesture of good will to the Soviet Union. None of the returnees spoke of their treatment or the conditions in the camps, however. I did ask one of our neighbor's children, whose father had just returned, but was told he had been cautioned not to speak of his incarceration on penalty of being returned to the camp.

During this time of uncertainty and confusion, Dad received notice to report for military service, though he was thirty-four and physically no match for the younger men in uniform. For us, his call came as a surprise, completely unexpected. Neither he nor mother nor I had given any thought to such a possibility during the days of growing tensions, although we should have anticipated it. There was no getting around it. He left, as the clouds of war were thickening and hanging low, when the time for second thoughts had passed us by.

5

War!

At the crack of dawn, on 1 September 1939, Hitler unleashed the Wehrmacht to crush any Polish resistance to his demands on Danzig and the corridor to East Prussia. He was determined to restore to the Reich the eastern territories that Germany had been forced to give up following its defeat in World War I. Within hours, planes of the Luftwaffe were bombing targets in and around Warsaw, the capital city. We were in a state of war. From the first news that morning, we were sitting near the radio listening intently to the latest reports from the front and everyone was talking about the events of the day. There was agreement that Germany was throwing everything in its arsenal at them; tanks by the hundreds, thousands of foot soldiers, squadrons of aircraft, and all the ships needed to ensure a swift victory. The Poles were in no position to respond decisively; Hitler had mobilized his forces quietly, and then launched a full-blown attack with the power and intensity of a bolt of lightning. The Poles were no match for the German steamroller. The advance quickly gained momentum as our troops took full advantage of the enemy's weaknesses.

Our country's instant success was somewhat marred when France and England declared war on Germany two days later. What we had envisioned as a short but powerful skirmish to set the Poles straight took on the prospect of an engagement of longer duration. Luck was on our side, though; the Western powers were

offering moral support and lip service to the Poles, but were
staying out of the fighting. The Wehrmacht, in turn, was on alert,
manning their positions in the fortifications and bunkers of the
West Wall facing France from Aachen to Baden.

The Poles had been pushed deep into their own territory when
the Soviet Army entered the war on 17 September and attacked
them from the rear. The Poles suddenly were faced with fighting a
war on two fronts, a condition that brought about their capitulation
just ten days later. While Soviet intervention may have helped
speed Poland's downfall, we at home could not comprehend the
basis of our alliance with them. There was mumbling that the
Russians were merely moving their sphere of influence closer to
Germany's borders.

While the Wehrmacht was prosecuting the land war, a U-Boat
of the Kriegsmarine made its first significant mark by sinking the
aircraft carrier *Courageous*, off southwestern Ireland. The British
lost 500 men in this single action. News of the sinking came via a
special radio announcement, followed with the playing of the
submariner's song, a tune every man, woman and child would
eventually know by heart. The sinking of the British battleship
Royal Oak at Scapa Flow on 14 October, was reason for additional
jubilation. In this action the British lost 833 men.

Rationing of food and staples was controlled via a system of
coupons the merchant would clip from coupon sheets presented
by the customer at the time of a purchase. At first, the system was
rather cumbersome; there were red coupons for bread, yellow for
butter and fats, green for milk, light blue for meats and meat
products, pink for wheat and rye products, such as flour, oatmeal
etc., and white for sugar and jams. Quantity entitlements were
based on the age of the coupon holder, with the quantity values of
the coupons being announced weekly on radio and in the papers.
Later in the war the quantities would be preprinted on the
coupons and the variety and color of the coupon sheets reduced
and simplified considerably.

Foodstuffs were now rigidly controlled and the rationing required changes in our diets and eating habits. There was whole
milk for babies and children, but skim milk for adults. And of
course, the milklady was accountable for the milk she had in her

cans on the wagon. She was required to turn in a coupon for every liter dispensed along her route. The baker was prohibited from selling freshly baked bread because it would not last. A 500-gram ration of warm, fresh bread would be gone in no time; the temptation to eat and enjoy would just be too great. However, after aging a day, rye bread would get solid and harden up. Then it had body and was also better for our teeth. So the rules seemed reasonable, but we still longed for a big hunk from a loaf just out of the oven. In the absence of butter, we dunked our bread in substitute coffee and then into a bowl of sugar. That could be a real treat when there was little else on the menu.

The purchase of a pair of shoes required a special permit from the town hall. The number of permits issued was based on the stock available in town, plus the need of the applicants. Our people had always been thrifty, but now they were required to make everything last several times longer. Cobblers were never out of work; there was always something to fix. A clothing card was also issued to each person for all manner of clothing; outerwear, underwear, socks, even suits and dresses. It was the owner's option to apply them toward a major item of clothing each year, or to satisfy the year-round needs for smaller items. There were not enough coupons to have it both ways.

Dad was discharged from military service by the end of October; he had been away for less than three months, just long enough to complete his basic training. The sides of his suitcase were stenciled: "Reserve hat Ruh," reserves are at rest. We were thrilled at his early release and happy to have him with us again. He didn't waste much time getting back to work. Through contacts he was able to secure a job at our *Gemeindeamt*, the town hall, in the new Rationing Office, issuing food ration cards and clothing permits.

We moved again soon after he got home. After making arrangements at the Rathskeller, the only hotel in town, we rented two rooms on the upper floor. There, we had a combination living room/kitchen with a small stove, and down the hall, a fairly large but unheated bedroom. Our bathroom was out in the hallway. Sometimes we ate in the restaurant downstairs in the hotel, but generally Mother would do the cooking in our small room, which was really not intended for such use. But we had to make do. The hotel was the best we could get on short notice when our landlord at the former porcelain factory asked us to leave, after he had collected enough in rental money to buy a motorcycle. The situation was discouraging; my folks had not thought greed and selfishness would still prevail in the New Germany.

Snow was plentiful that winter. Whenever the town's horse-drawn snowplow came up the street, several of us boys hurried to meet the rig so we could volunteer our weight as extra balast. We loved riding the plow; it was a lot of fun even if our fingers, ears and noses were freezing and had to be thawed out later in front of a fire. There were hardly any cars in town, only a few delivery trucks and an occasional bus, so things were generally quiet on the main thoroughfare. The icy winds that were blowing that time of year turned the street into a sheet of ice and a ready-made ice-skating rink for us youngsters. Our skates came in handy when chores in the lower part of town had to be taken care of; they allowed us to get around faster. For a fast and hair-raising sleigh-ride we would hustle up the hill to the Parson's house and come flying down the incline and across the main street before we would be able to come to a stop. Oh, how Mother yelled out the window when she caught us making that dangerous run.

When snow drifts blocked the roads leading out of town, the men were called out, many of them members of the S.A., the brown-shirts, to manually clear away the drifts and open up the country roads leading into the village. All clearing was done by hand; it was hard work, and Mother sometimes had me take a hot drink to Dad and his comrades on the detail, so they'd get something warm into their stomachs.

Except for the rationing, and the fact that some of the men in our neighborhood had been drafted, there was little to give us the feeling that we were at war that winter. We listened to reports on radio and read about the war in the newspapers, but everything seemed so far away.

The lull ended on 9 April 1940, when our troops swept into Denmark, and a combined air and sea landing was made at key points in Norway, bringing those countries under German occupation. We were all cheers knowing we had prevented the British from gaining a foothold in the countries to our north. Even though fighting continued in Norway for weeks, we knew that campaign, too, would turn into another victory for the Reich.

On 10 May, however, it seemed like the war had just started, this time with even greater force. Our victory over Poland, the taking of Denmark and the rapid advance in Norway all seemed dwarfed by the magnitude of the operations launched that day. German ground and paratroops hit Holland, Belgium and Luxembourg simultaneously, extending their attack to French territory just two days later. We were kept apprised by radio of the fierce fighting on the entire western front. Our submarine operations were picking up and now British planes were dropping their bomb loads on our cities in the Ruhr area.

War was in full swing, but everything was progressing in our favor. Holland capitulated within a few days, with Belgium following suit on 28 May. At the same time some 350,000 men of the British Expeditionary Forces were trying to save their necks at Dunkirk. Though many were evacuated, our armed forces succeeded in wiping out much of the British arsenal right on the beaches. At our Youth meetings we were all fired up knowing the British had to hightail it back to their island, where they belonged. The subsequent all-out assault on French forces, and the inevitable capitulation that followed, gave us a renewed sense of pride in Germany's military. Oh, how we admired the soldiers when they came home on furlough; we couldn't wait to corner these heroes to learn of their combat experiences and exploits.

During this time we received permission to move into a vacant two-room apartment upstairs in the old brewery, at the Markt Platz, just across the street from the Rathskeller. As it turned out, we were required to share a five-room apartment with another family, but we had our own kitchen and bedroom. And although we used the same front door and shared the toilet facilities with the other family, we were pretty much on our own.

While my folks were concerning themselves with furnishing our new place, I was tending cows in the meadows outside of town, and helping the farmer gather up his hay. I always looked forward to the sandwiches and Ersatz-Kaffee, (the commonly used coffee substitute) his wife would bring while we were out in the fields; I felt so free and lucky, sitting there and enjoying those sandwiches with wurst or goose fat, at a time when food was in short supply. Working for a farmer made all the difference; they were almost self-supporting and the rationing system didn't really affect them. I was always there, helping to bring in the harvest of rye, wheat, oats, turnips and kohlrabi and, later, even the potato crop. It was hard work, but the farmer paid well, in flour and potatoes; that helped us all around. Sometimes he would hand me a bag of eggs to take home; that's when Mother showed off her cake-making skills. And when there were no crops to harvest, the farmer would have me clean out the cow barn and his horse stables. This meant tossing manure onto one of his wagons, and from there onto the manure pile. It was a dirty and smelly job, but worth all the inconveniences; food for work was a good system.

From time to time I worked for the baker in the lower part of the village, delivering hot rolls early in the morning; that was fun as long as the weather was nice. My hand wagon loaded to the top, I made my way up the street, stopping frequently to drop off the orders while picking up the food coupons and the money. On my return to the bakery I could expect to receive some rolls or a loaf of bread to take home, along with my pay. When the butcher needed help I would help clean up the slaughterhouse, restock the showcases, or wet-mop the tiled floors. Oftentimes I would net a bag of sausage ends and other shop leftovers which Mother quickly converted into another meal.

Meanwhile, the war had escalated to the point where the British were bombing German cities at night, including places like Hamburg, Bremen and even Berlin, while German planes were engaging in highly destructive bombing strikes on London. Our blitz continued for many months, with British cities being battered relentlessly. We had high hopes that England would sooner or later give in, now that much of Europe had been brought under the swastika, and our bombers were inflicting harrowing blows on her cities. Instead, the British initiated even more powerful air strikes against Germany by mid-December.

A blackout was in place, but enforcement became strict only after the British began penetrating deeper into German airspace. Our air raid warden started to walk the streets right after dusk and whistled or would throw a stone at our windows if the least bit of light, even a slight hairline, could be seen. The air raid siren, installed on the roof of the school next door to our house, was tested occasionally to ensure it worked properly, and also to familiarize the people with the various signals and what they meant. We were getting ready for any eventuality, even in small towns like ours, deep in the heartlands of Germany.

The following February, our troops landed in North Africa to help our Axis partner, the Italians, who were suffering severe setbacks at the hands of the British. The men of the Afrika Korps, in their sun helmets and khaki uniforms, made a tremendous impression on the members of the Youth. We saw in them an elite force, made up of some of the finest young soldiers Germany could muster. They were sharp, and Erwin Rommel, their leading general, quickly became a living legend. The Panzer song, with its refrain "Panzer rollen in Afrika vor," became one of our favorite tunes. Seldom would our Youth group march through town without at least once singing this stirring song. Then there was the melody dedicated to the Luftwaffe that ended: "Bomben, Bomben, Bomben auf Engeland." It too had a special place on the top of our list of marching songs. For every campaign, for every special occasion or circumstance, we would learn a stirring new song by heart. They would put us in a fighting mood or trance. We just marched along, singing our hearts out, loud and clear; there was little doubt in our minds that "today Germany belongs to us, and tomorrow, the whole world."

Because of his skiing and mountain climbing experience, Uncle Erich was assigned to a *Gebirgsjaeger* Regiment. On his last furlough home, he mentioned having been aboard a ship in the harbor of Cuxhaven, on the North Sea, waiting to be transported and landed in England as part of a planned invasion, but that the action had been called off because information on the assault had been leaked to the British. Enemy bombing of the harbor and the ships at anchor rendered the operation untenable.

He didn't have too many months to wait, however, until he got his chance to see action. Erich, a Lieutenant by then, was among the assault echelon on 6 April, spearheading Germany's attack on Greece. One of the first across the border, he was mortally wounded and bled to death on the battlefield.

By the end of the month, the armies of Greece and Yugoslavia as well had been destroyed. Germany attacked the Soviet Union on 22 June 1941, barely two 2 months after the Balkans had been secured. This was perhaps the greatest military operation ever; more than three million troops assaulted Russia on a solid front from the Arctic to the Black Sea with hundreds of thousands of vehicles and even larger numbers of horses, plus 3,500 tanks, and close to 2,000 planes. Our patriotic song of the time, was: "Von Finland bis zum Schwarzen Meer, Vorwaerts," from Finland to the Black Sea, onward, onward. The numbers given over the radio for Russians captured and for vehicles and tanks destroyed during the first weeks was beyond anyone's comprehension. It was as though entire divisions of Soviet troops were wiped out. We knew our assault could be nothing other than colossal. But we couldn't understand what went wrong with the German-Russian alliance that had existed during the Poland campaign. It was hard to figure out. Maybe it was because Russia insisted on taking the Baltic states and entering into alliances that ran counter to the Fuehrer's plans. We didn't know.

Dad was recalled to military service and assigned to a veterinary unit in Rastenburg, East Prussia, requisitioning horses for the Wehrmacht. While on leave he told us that his *Heimatpferdepark* would relocate to another city, as a Fuehrer headquarters was being established near his garrison town and all available space was being taken over to support the new complex. It was difficult for me to understand how Hitler could be shuttling back and forth between Berlin and Rastenburg, when he would be needed at both places at the same time.

Earlier in the year, Dad had enrolled me at the *Oberschule* for boys in Werdau; now I travelled daily to the city by bus, or walked the four kilometers. In winter, there would be times when I would have to resort to getting there on skis. My best classes were English, and my American slang soon became a persistent and nagging headache for Studienrat Fleischer, our English teacher. Whenever it was time to read aloud from the textbook, Frohberger, my classmate, nudged me in the hope I would raise my hand and volunteer to do the reading. He waited for me to slaughter a word or two with my slang. For the amusement of my classmates I often obliged, particularly when I could do a job on words like "half" and "aunt." Herr Fleischer took it lightly at first, correcting my pronunciation, but realized in time that we were trying to annoy him. For punishment I repeatedly had to stay over and write a thousand times, "I shall pronounce my words correctly." That's when the fun ended.

When I wore my knickerbockers and the cap I had brought with me from America, the kids would make fun of me. They would come running and pull at the bottoms of my knickerbockers, calling them *Pumphosen,* girly bloomers, then grab for my cap and toss it around the school yard. They called my cap a *Schlaeger-muetze,* a gangster's cap, because it was made like the caps worn by American criminals as depicted in photos they had seen. I thought how strange it was to be popular one moment and to be picked on the next. At times like this I was very unhappy, having to put up with the teasing, but deep down I knew I would show up some of the toughs one day.

In our history and geography classes we covered the storm of the Huns from the east, and quickly proclaimed our attack on Russia a defensive measure; we were merely anticipating and destroying the Mongolian hordes before they could invade all of Europe. We felt we were now destined to protect Western civilization, including our present enemies, by fighting what we saw as an unavoidable battle.

As part of our national-political education, we were exposed to repeated criticisms of the Church, one of the milestones of our continuing indoctrination into the philosophy of National Socialism. Our teacher ridiculed the collection boxes inside the churches by saying, "As soon as the money jingles in the box, your soul jumps into heaven." We laughed at his jokes. The seeds he was planting were beginning to sprout, however.

Chemistry was challenging, especially the discussions on the origins and making of gun powder. I didn't miss a word, watching and listening intently as our teacher performed his experiments. It didn't take long before I began to stage my own experiments in our dingy cellar, where I managed to accidentally blow up my test tubes. That ended my unsupervised experimenting.

One day, I was called out of class and told to report to the conference room where a team of recruiters from the Adolf Hitler School was waiting to see me. Oh, no, not me, I thought. One of my classmates was already at the school; he was very unhappy. He couldn't keep up academically, although he was an ace in sports. I hesitated at the prospect of being selected and having to go through the misery of not being able to keep up physically. The thought of graduating from the A. H. School was very enticing, however; it would open doors and almost certainly, guarantee a later career.

I was asked a number of general questions about myself by the team members, and also, where my father was and what he was doing. I told them he was an acting first sergeant in the Wehrmacht, but couldn't remember the name of the place where he was stationed. I hemmed and hawed; I could feel my face turning red. I just couldn't remember. I was embarrassed. "You may leave now," said the interviewer crisply, and not a moment too soon, as far as I am concerned. He was annoyed with my hesitant replies. I, in turn, couldn't wait to get down the stairs and back into my classroom. After this, anything was better than being selected for the A. H. School. My daily Vitamin C pill was waiting for me on my desk. Oh, how I needed some energy right now, and the taste of orange was so refreshing after that ordeal with the recruiters.

Even though our troops were moving along in Russia and nearing Moscow, they didn't get into the city before cold weather set in. Our army was getting bogged down and preparing for a Russian winter. We couldn't help thinking of Napoleon and the foray that had ended in disaster for his army; would our Wehrmacht experience the same fate? Doubtful, even though our forces were falling back in certain areas to consolidate their lines.

The Japanese, who were militarily aligned with Germany, attacked Pearl Harbor on 7 December 1941. That would keep the Americans busy, we thought. Now perhaps, the flow of war supplies from America would slow down, and the Tommies would be unable to continue fighting. But, on 11 December, Hitler declared war on the United States. This could change the situation. We knew America was a big country, with vast resources, but we could not assess just how powerful and capable the Americans really were. Nor did we know they had the wherewithal to carry on a war in the Pacific after their initial heavy losses and still keep supplying England. We were confident the Fuehrer had it all under control.

Shortly after, Aunt Edith returned from America with her husband Werner. At their formal welcoming in Berlin, they were told a submarine of the Kriegsmarine had followed their ship all the way across the Atlantic, right to Spain where they disembarked and were put on a train for Berlin. Later, when Edith joined us in Fraureuth, she recalled seeing a periscope in the water not far from their ship every now and then, confirming the information given them by the U-Boat commander.

One day, a friend of mine—also named Werner—came running to our house to tell of an object he had seen falling from the sky, just about the time a Messerschmitt 109 was flying over. I followed him up the path next to the church and to the fields beyond. After a fifteen-minute hike we came to the little pond where we had tried out and lost my submersible toy submarine a while back. It had been my fault. I had always attached a long string to it before I wound up the motor and let it go; this time I just set the rudder to make it go in a circle and come back to me, but it must have become entangled in the weeds growing in the pond. I felt bad about that loss; it had been a neat submarine, and a toy I could not replace.

"Over there," Werner lead the way to the object; it was the canopy from a ME-109 fighter. We wondered why the pilot would have ejected the canopy; maybe he was getting ready to bail out; maybe his plane had been hit; or maybe he had developed engine trouble. We would never know. The canopy was not heavy; it was made of an aluminum framework that held plexiglass panes in place. We each grabbed one end and carried our trophy to town, where Werner reported our find to the police.

A year or two later, he was an apprentice at the *Wagonfabrik* where they were making trucks and painting them up in a tan camouflage pattern, for the Afrika Korps. As his welding project, he made a model 88mm antiaircraft gun and gave it to me to use with the hundreds of toy soldiers I had. It looked exactly like the real thing; it was just too bad it couldn't be fired. I kept it for the longest time and even used it instead as a toy machine-pistol when some of us played soldiers.

During the spring of 1942, the campaign in Russia went slowly; our equipment and tanks were getting stuck in pools of mud, while the Soviets were hitting our forces hard wherever they could. They were resorting to partisan warfare, waylaying convoys in isolated areas. Fighting in Russia had become a battle of nerves, with many casualties. It was hitting home, and hard. Many a family in town had lost loved ones during the first winter, when our armies were in desperate need of warm clothing and were disabled by the cold. We had been busy, helping collect blankets, sweaters, warm boots, long underwear, anything a soldier could wear to help keep warm. Much of this relief, the things donated by the people, did not reach the front in time to do much good. We hoped for better times in the coming year.

Time had rolled around for me to register in the senior branch of the Hitler Youth. I had turned fourteen. Dad had managed to get a furlough about that time, and he accompanied me when I reported to the Buergermeister's office for the mandatory registration. I stepped up to the desk where a town clerk and a uniformed Hitler Youth leader asked a series of questions, like my name, address, etc.

"Birthplace?" snapped the clerk.

"Pawtucket."

"Say it again."

"Pawtucket."

"Never heard that name before." He paused, writing down the information, and then asked, "Confession?"

I felt confused. I had never been baptized. It had been my father's belief that I could choose a religion according to my own beliefs when I was older. But now they wanted to know for the Youth record what I believed in. I didn't know what to say. The clerk looked at me, clarifying, "Gottglaeubig oder Deutschglaeubig?" He wanted to know if I believed in God or in Germany. My family never went to church in Germany and seldom spoke of God, except for referring to the great super-human power that watched over us, as the "Almighty," and the "Super Intelligence." Everyone believed in Germany, though, everyone was solidly behind the Fuehrer, so I said, "Deutschglaeubig," looking at my father, who nodded approvingly. When the registration process had been completed, I was handed the card to review. I grinned as I read the entries; the clerk had recorded my birthplace as "Bad Dagged." Maybe he knew where it was, but I didn't.

Even though I was now registered with the Hitler Youth, I stayed on with the Jungvolk organization to lead the *Fanfarenzug*, our band of fanfares and bass drums. I had belonged since it was formed in 1939. We were always up front in the column when the local youth group marched through town, sounding off with the kind of marching tunes that would keep our followers in step. It was fun. People stopped on the street, watching and listening when we came along; we knew they were proud of us.

During my school vacation that summer, Dad arranged for me to stay with a farmer in the town of Schwaegerau, East Prussia, just a few kilometers from Insterburg, where he was now stationed. The river Pregel flowed by, behind the farmhouse, which allowed me to make swimming a part of my daily routine. Herr Dehn, the farmer, also ran a *Bierstube*, the local tavern, in his house, and I was given the responsibility of filling empty snap-top bear bottles with the brew that was delivered to him in barrels. Dad visited on weekends. He came in a one-of-a-kind horse and buggy. The men of his unit had taken an old car and transformed it into a smooth riding buggy with air-inflated tires. Of course, it was painted field-grey; it belonged to the Wehrmacht. We took it on a long ride through woods and swamp, and we talked. I wondered if this section of East Prussia might have been the place where the Czar's army had been driven into the swamps in World War I. Dad gave me the impression that we were in the fringe areas of that battle.

On the farm, I helped out turning and bringing in the hay, and also received my first lessons in milking cows. I hated it. I couldn't get much milk, and then the cows would wallop me with their tails, to the amusement of Herr Dehn. He was a strict but good man who held the position of local farmers' leader. He mainly left me to myself while I was working. The only other people about my age were two Lithuanian girls—employed on the farm as maids—who ogled me and even sang songs when I came near where they were working. Although I was becoming inquisitive about the opposite sex, under no circumstances could I get too friendly with anyone from the East; that was against the rules and the teachings about the separation of races.

By the end of June, Rommel's Afrika Korps had taken Tobruk, where my cousin Paul lost his life. Reports reaching us advised of the defeat of Britain's Eighth Army, while German forces in Russia were in the Crimea and on their way to the Caucasus mountains. The 19 August landing of an Allied force in excess of 6,000 men at Dieppe, and their prompt annihilation on the beaches, lead us to believe our troops had repulsed the invasion of mainland Europe. Once again we were cheering a great victory. Newspapers displayed the sheet music and text of the British song "We shall hang our wash up on the Siegfried Line," with an overprint of wounded British soldiers marching into captivity as prisoners of war. This time the British had gotten it bad; half of their landing force were dead, wounded or captured. By the closing days of 1942 and right into the early days of 1943, however, the German Sixth Army under General von Paulus was facing almost certain annihilation at Stalingrad, where in excess of a quarter of a million men were surrounded by the Soviets. This turn of events struck a heavy blow to our pride and confidence, as did the news that the Afrika Korps was now under heavy Allied attack in Libya as well as in Tunisia.

We were told that troops on the Russian front were resorting to placing newspapers under their jackets and sweaters, and lining their boots in the same manner, to keep from freezing. We knew then that things were rough on the Russian front, and that our soldiers had to fight more than just enemy troops to stay alive, let alone to hold the line. We at home struggled in our own way to stay healthy and keep strong. A horsemeat dish for the Sunday dinner table was a real treat. We could get double the normal meat allotment if we choose to buy horsemeat instead of regular meat or wurst products. That was a good way to fill growling stomachs.

Mother had to be creative to stretch our meager provisions. One time she did such a good job preparing a big pot of Hungarian Goulash for Dad when he came home on furlough that he was all praises. The flavor of the meat in the thick tasty gravy, combined with *Gruene Kloese*, the potato-balls she made only on special occasions, made a meal fit for a king. She couldn't keep a secret, however, and when she told him he had eaten horsemeat, he was sick to his stomach. He loved horses, and more so now, being assigned to a military horse park that acquired thousands of these animals for service with units of the Wehrmacht. People like him protected and babied their horses; they were like comrades in arms. To eat one of them was upsetting, and quite a shock for Dad. Later, though, we all laughed. He couldn't deny Mother had cooked up a masterpiece.

One of our neighbors, home on furlough, gave me a Polish helmet he had brought back, after I begged and nagged him for it. I wanted it so much, a real enemy helmet; what a prize! Oh, how lucky I was. It was so different from the Wehrmacht helmets. Now I wanted more. Soon after, I was given a French helmet. Though I wanted it badly, and added it to my collection, there was dried blood on it that made me pull a face; something prevented me from handling it freely and enjoying my latest acquisition. That didn't deter me, however, and my new hobby didn't end there. Through word of mouth, I was able to pick up another helmet or two, and even an outdated rifle. In our neighborhood we played with these things a lot; now we could recognize our enemies by the helmets we were wearing. Before long, however, the time for play grew short, and I stashed my treasures away under the rafters in the peak of the roof above the attic, where no one would ever look.

When General von Paulus finally surrendered his forces at Stalingrad on 2 February, we were in a state of shock, although we had been expecting disappointing news for some time. We lost close to a quarter of a million men; the entire Sixth Army was wiped out. And all the lost equipment was irreplaceable. This was the saddest day ever, a day of sorrow and mourning. What did this defeat mean? Would Stalin's forces follow up with an offensive, pouring through the break in our lines, to encircle our troops in adjacent areas? Would new Mongolian hordes from beyond the Urals be unleashed to overrun and destroy our Western civilization? Could we hold them in place? On the home front, we felt lost, in a state of disbelief. What would happen now?

We got our answer on 18 February, when Joseph Goebbels,

the Reich's propaganda minister, made an emotional speech at the overcrowded *Sportspalast* in Berlin before 15,000 followers, challenging Germany and the people, and setting the stage for what he called "Total War." He advocated drastic measures and extreme sacrifices from every man, woman and child. His speech was hypnotizing and put us in a renewed trance; it was a boost to our faltering willpower and gave us a new sense of direction. Spontaneous calls from the audience made us shiver as we listened to the words over the radio: "Fuehrer command, and we will follow!" Goebbels' concluding appeal said it all: "Nun, Volk, steh auf und Sturm brich los!" Now, people, stand up, and let the storm break loose! We were at Total War, ready to fight with everything we had.

Our Youth training program had been tough and thorough all along, but now we were beginning to realize the seriousness of the times and that our personal survival would depend on how well we mastered the subjects we were being taught. Rifle training was introduced at this time. Everyone loved it; learning to take a rifle apart and reassemble it as fast as a soldier gave us a positive feeling of accomplishment. Though practice firing was only with BB guns at first, and later with small bore rifles, for most of us this was our first exposure firing a weapon with live ammunition. What a thrill, learning to handle and aim a gun properly, and hit the center of the target.

Night compass marches through the woods were troublesome in the beginning, especially when our leaders let us walk right past the designated check-in points only a few meters away from the compass route we had plotted for ourselves. Several times we got lost in the thicket of the forest and didn't return to our homes until 4:00 a.m., when we should have returned by midnight. Our leaders just let us continue on blindly, while they went home. They wanted to teach us a lesson: accuracy in reading the compass. We learned quickly and gained much self confidence.

Camouflage training and field exercises were also high on our list of priorities. Every second Saturday, our *Faehnlein* would be split into two units, Blue and Red. Each youth—there were about 100 of us—tied a colored ribbon above his elbow over his left uniform sleeve to identify the group he belonged to. One group headed for the woods to build a fort of felled trees and branches that it would later defend against the second group, which moved out about an hour later. In the intervening time, the second group studied maps and became familiar with the lay of the land where the fort would be located. The map-reading instructions we had received earlier came in very handy at times like this.

We would quickly pick out gulleys and other depressions in the ground that could be followed to approach the enemy without being noticed. Sometimes that meant crawling on our bellies for long distances, or advancing in short leaps without making any noise, and forever seeking the cover of a bush or tree trunk. We never knew what the first group's plans were. There were times when they would place outposts along our anticipated route of advance. Some of their boys would be lying fully camouflaged under fallen pine branches, or they might be hunching in a small indentation in the ground, waiting to ambush us and tear the colored ribbon from our arms, which meant we had been killed or immobilized. Once the scouts of the second group spotted the fort, the unit quietly surrounded the area, and at the sound of the troop leader's whistle, they charged the fort with cheers of "Hurrah." The only way to get the ribbon from the opponent's sleeve was to jump him, wrestle him to the ground and hope to yank the ribbon from him before he took yours. The fighting got rough at times, and some of the boys went home showing off bruises they had sustained in battle. To them, the scars were signs of their early manhood.

During an overnight camp-out in the woods of Teichwolframs-dorf, on the far side of the Werdauer Wald, our *Faehnlein* was harassed most of the night by others, who were shouting from behind the trees in the dark, threatening our safety. Our leaders let it be known that the display was not pre-arranged, and that we were to remain with our comrades near the tents. We did as we were told, for we did not know what might be lurking out there in the dark. There had been talk of the existence of a dissident youth group called the "Edelweiss Piraten," but I just could not believe there really was such a group, and certainly not in our area. Why would anyone be against the system, and if they were, why would they want to risk arrest and prosecution? Now, under the Total

War principles, they had everything to lose, and absolutely nothing to gain.

In mid-May we received more disheartening news. This time it was from North Africa, where the Afrika Korps was forced to finally surrender. This took another quarter of a million men out of action, Germans and Italians combined. I knew we couldn't stand many more losses like this.

To become more self-sufficient, Mom and I would often go to the woods before daybreak, looking for mushrooms. I had learned how to tell the good ones from the bad, and where to look for them in the forest. The telltale little mounds of pine needles in damp places, near a creek or body of water, gave away where the new ones were popping through the ground, looking for a place in the sun. It was always best to catch them while they were still covered with pine needles; that way we could be sure they were fresh. We usually brought back enough so that Mother could cook up some for a meal and dry the others to save for a bowl of delicious mushroom soup some other day. There were also times when we walked the woods looking for blueberries. We were lucky most of the time, which meant another batch of Mother's delicious blueberry pudding.

We hauled firewood home from the lower part of town, in my hand wagon. It was always pretty heavy, pulling the loaded wagon all the way up town, and quite a relief when the trip was over. Once in a while we were lucky enough to receive a permit to buy a whole meter of wood from a farmer, who would deliver it to us in a horse-drawn wagon. All I had to do then was to get it into our shed in back of the house and stack it up. Later, I could chop it into smaller pieces with an axe, as needed. We had to haul our own coal and brickets in the hand wagon, the same as for the firewood. When coal was available, we would be allotted one or two hundred weights at a time. Mom sometimes came along with me to get it; she pulled and I pushed the loaded wagon through the village, and then we unloaded the bags by the bucket-full, to get it all down the stairs and into the cellar. The dire shortage of gasoline was manifest in the appearance of more and more wood-burning trucks; even the Wehrmacht began to use this type of vehicle. My friends and I thought the wood-burners were a great idea; another masterpiece of our country's ingenuity, and evidence that we really did have the answers to most problems.

The existing food shortages, combined with the rationing system, prevented restaurants from offering much in the way of prepared meals. The restaurant in the railroad station in Werdau, however, came up with the idea of making meatless soups available to the travelers. Most of the time they offered *Krautsuppe*, at a very reasonable price. The soup was made mostly of cabbage, potatoes, onions and some other readily available vegetables, plus a variety of spices, and a plate of it was always welcome. Mother encouraged me to stop there on my way home from school, and for a time, stopping at the railroad station for my plate of soup became a daily ritual. I could have my soup while waiting for the bus to Fraureuth, and Mother could delay our suppers until later in the evening when I got hungry again.

Daily life had become highly stressful. The Americans had begun to make deep incursions into the airspace of the Reich with their bomber formations. The British had been doing so for some time, but they made most of their bomb runs during the night. The Americans were now resorting to daylight bombing. We joked at first that the Americans needed the light of day to figure out where they were going, and to find their way back to their bases. We felt that the British had acquired their night bombing skills through months of experience, but that the Americans still had a lot to learn. We did agree among ourselves, however, that daylight runs were tougher and much more dangerous; not only could our fighters make visual contact, but the flak batteries deployed along the flightpath of the intruders could also zero in more easily on targets they could see.

Our jokes about the Americans were short-lived, however. They were bold in their actions, and seemed to have endless supplies of fuel, plus the necessary aircraft to keep up a relentless pressure on our economy and our people. The Fatherland was being bombed somewhere every day. And during the night, some of the places hit earlier in the day would get a double dose. We could expect the siren on top of the school to start howling during daytime hours whenever enemy bombers were approaching critical targets in central Germany. The same could be expected during nighttime hours. More frequently, we would be driven to our air raid shelters during the night, while the thunder of Allied planes high in the sky above kept us on edge for what seemed like eternity. During the overflights, we huddled in our cold cellar, hoping the bombers would not spot any lights and would keep going. Nights were often restless, spent wondering if the siren would go off, and mighty short, when it did begin to howl with an ear-piercing, vibrating tone. We would then have to get out of bed and there would be no returning to the apartment for at least three hours. It was usually two or three o'clock in the morning by then. And when there were two alerts in a single night, we would not get any sleep at all, making us all feel cranky and worn out the next day, grown-ups and younger people alike.

Through the Youth movement, I was assigned to the town hall as a messenger, on standby during nighttime alerts. This required me to put on my uniform every time the siren went off during the night, and hop on my bike and hustle to the lower part of the village in the dark to report for duty. I would stay until needed, or until the all clear was sounded. From in front of the building, I could see brightly lit target markers that enemy scouting planes had set off in the distance. The array of lights looked much like Christmas trees, which is what we called them.

Throughout the years, treks of refugees were constantly making their way westward through town. The caravans consisted of horse-drawn wagons loaded to the brim with whatever possessions their owners had been able to salvage from their bombed-out homes. One day one of these caravans was on the open road out of town, traveling in the direction of Greiz, just as an American bomber formation flew almost directly overhead. The whistling of bombs could be heard in the village. We came running into the street to see what was going on. There were explosions in the distance, and the thundering sound was loud enough to be no more than a few kilometers away.

Curiosity prompted a few of us youngsters to dash across the street and up the hill past the parson's house, into the fields beyond the village. We ran in the direction of the explosions we'd heard. In the distance we could see the caravan of covered wagons moving along as though nothing had happened. We thought for sure the bombs had been meant for them. We kept running. "There—the field ahead—it looks all chewed up," one of the boys shouted. When we reached the spot, we counted several huge bomb craters. We had not seen anything like that before. Why did they bomb the open field, when the caravan of wagons was on the road less than a kilometer away? The bombardier either missed the target, or was in a hurry to unload whatever bombs he still had on board, not caring where they would fall; the route the planes had taken lead us to believe they were on their way home. We would never know the real answer.

We scoured the area for duds and bomb splinters. We found both. There was a hole in the ground, in line with several craters; it looked for sure like an unexploded bomb. There were big chunks of ragged steel lying around, splinters of the bomb casings that had flown through the air following the explosions. We didn't want to chance staying in the area too long, so we quickly gathered up a few splinters and headed back to the village. Not many of the grown-ups waiting for us had seen bomb splinters before, so we showed off our booty and then told the police about the impact area and that there might also be a few duds around.

As a defensive measure against radar detection by German ground stations, the Allied bomber formations dropped large quantities of tinfoil strips along their flight paths; these strips would land on fields and crops. Not knowing if the foil strips were "clean" or if they had been impregnated with phosphorous—which might ignite—the civil authorities called out the Youth to make a sweep across the fields to pick up and bag the strips and to report any other strange objects that might be spotted along the way. The youths were alerted not to touch any toys they might find in the fields, as the enemy was dropping playthings that had explosive charges in them. The Hitler Youth was also called out whenever leaflets had been dropped; we were ordered to search and clear the area of the unwanted propaganda flyers. Circulating such leaflets among the population was a serious offense that officials would not tolerate; therefore, early collection was in everyone's interest.

One day I was given a small parachute that someone found in a nearby field; it was made of red silk and measured about thirty-five to forty centimeters in diameter. It undoubtedly had served some purpose for the enemy bombers that were daily plying our skies. The chute was really neat and small enough to play with, so I soon tied one of my toy soldiers to it to see if I could convert and modernize my little land army to include parachutists. The chute worked well; it took my toy soldier all the way across the Markt Platz, drifting slowly in the wind. My friend Werner suggested tying the four corners of a handkerchief to the tail of a kite, then rolling up the parachute with the toy soldier and placing it in the sling formed by the handkerchief. When the kite was high enough in the air, Werner said, we could yank the string so the tail would bob up and down until the red parachute dropped out—and, hopefully, it would open. I thought it was a great idea, so we tried it, and it worked perfectly. That was not good enough for us, however; we wanted to experiment further. On our next trip to the fields, we looked for hamsters and field mice, and managed to snag a mama mouse. We tied her to the parachute and launched her on a voyage, drifting high above the fields. The breeze moved the chute through the air pretty fast. We ran across potato, turnip, and kohlrabi fields, tripping and falling, always keeping that little red umbrella in sight. When we caught up with it, we found the mama mouse alive but exhausted; she had done well for us, so we untied her and let her go.

Enemy aircraft made their deepest penetration into Germany on 17 August, when 300 or more bombers attacked the city of Schweinfurt. Considerable damage was inflicted on ball bearing production facilities. Our consolation was that they lost sixty of their planes, a heavy price to pay; perhaps they would question the wisdom of such attacks in the future. But the Americans were persistent. They came back to Schweinfurt in mid-October with 230 bombers, and lost another sixty; but Germany's ball bearing production capability had suffered immensely. The need for alternative production sites became a very serious and critical issue, and soon afterwards, our idle and empty porcelain factory was set up to produce some of the war-essential products for the Kugel Fischer factory that had been wiped out in Schweinfurt. Following the establishment of the new facility, Mother, who had been working part-time for a vegetable distribution enterprise on the ground floor of our house, received notice to report for work at the Kugel Fischer plant in town. For her, Total War had arrived.

In September, the Italians surrendered a few days after the Allies invaded Southern Italy. Sicily had been taken earlier. In our Youth group we always mocked the Italians, our Axis partners. It all started with their own situation reports from North Africa, as given out by their High Command. We laughed at such statements as the capture of five machine guns and twelve British soldiers. Compared to the reports from the Oberkommando of the Wehrmacht, which documented the thousands of Russians captured and the hundreds of tanks destroyed, the Italians did not impress us at all.

Following the Allied landings, a new song was circulated for our Youth group to pick up and sing, in an effort to even further belittle the faltering Italians. The words "We are brave Italians; our realm is forever shrinking; Sicily they have taken; on the mainland they have come . . ." rang out loud and clear as the Jungvolk column strutted through the village on the following Saturday afternoon. Now Germany was dependent on its own resources and muscle to halt the Allied advance up the boot of Italy. On the eastern front, in turn, the Soviets were counterattacking and keeping the pressure on our troops, who were facing another dreadful Russian winter.

During the last weeks of 1943 our class at the *Oberschule* was notified that the Total War concept provided for the conscription of high school students who had reached their fifteenth birthday for military support services. That's me, I thought; I was fifteen in March. Most of the boys in my class were my age, so there was a good possibility that we might be drafted as a group; certainly that was something to hope for. Just before Christmas we were given our physicals and advised to be prepared to do service as Luftwaffenhelfer, away from home, and to anticipate our call-up in the very near future.

6

Soldiers at 15

Oberbuergermeister Uhlig of Werdau issued our draft notices on 8 January 1944, with instructions to report in front of the Railroad Station at 7:15 on the morning of 12 February. Even though we had been expecting the call-up any day after Christmas, we felt we hadn't been given much time; the interval between the issue and the reporting dates was shorter than we had expected. We still had a few days in school, which were filled with excitement and anticipation. About twenty of the twenty-four boys in our class had received their orders; all were born in 1928, so most of us were fifteen. We were being called to assist the Luftwaffe by performing support functions with an antiaircraft battery.

Though I was as fired-up as my classmates at the idea of going away and serving as a group, the statements the Reichsjugendfuehrer had made to the Jungvolk members attending the Rudolstadt encampment not long before, did not agree with what was happening. He had told us that England had started to draft children but that Germany had no need for similar action. Yet, here we were. Well, I thought, if the British youths could do it, so could we.

There was no doubt in our minds that we would all be at the station at the designated date and time, yet the small print on the back of the draft paper cautioned parents that they were subject to arrest if the student failed to report as ordered. During an earlier briefing of students and parents the term "sedition" had been used in connection with any parent's failure to cooperate. I couldn't understand why such strict warnings were being given when everyone was doing his duty for the Fatherland. It almost seemed that there was an element of distrust, a fear that people might actually object, or refuse to let their children go to war; but that was hard to believe.

As Luftwaffenhelfer, we were slated to wear the blue-grey uniform of the Flieger-HJ, the aviation branch of the youth movement, including the Hitler Youth armband. To distinguish our assignment to the Luftwaffe, we would wear a special triangular patch above our right front uniform pocket showing the Luftwaffe eagle and the letters "LH," for Luftwaffenhelfer. We envisioned the "LH" patch as a prestigious symbol since only students from high and middle schools were being called up, not students from trade schools or from among other groups undergoing apprenticeship training. We could already see ourselves as a special fraternity, a brotherhood of young soldiers.

What we didn't realize until much later was that people sarcastically interpreted the "LH" to mean "Letzte Hoffnung," last hope. Remarks along those lines did not go over too well with us; neither did the prescribed wearing of the Hitler Youth armband. In our minds, we were soldiers now, and no longer members of the Youth. After all, we were going to perform duties normally carried out by military personnel; that made us soldiers, too. We would not be going around collecting money for the poor and clothing for the Russian front any more; those days were over. Even before our reporting date, we knew we'd wear the armband only when members of the HJ Streifendienst, the Youth police patrol, were in the area. Usually, they patrolled the downtown sections of cities, and railroad stations. The only time we would really have to watch ourselves would be whenever we got a chance to go home, something we didn't think would happen too often, anyway.

Our parents were not thrilled with the idea of sending us into areas where the potential of being bombed would be many times greater than in the rural communities where most of us were living. Besides, KLV was relocating children from bombed cities to the safety of our area, while we were being fingered to man guns in primary target areas. There were rumblings of discontent, but none of the parents dared challenge the draft orders.

For us, the draftees, it truly was "the time of the young soldiers," as we often sang, marching through our towns and villages. The government saw to it, however, that time would be provided so we could continue our education while away from home, even though actual classroom hours were to be cut to eighteen hours per week, to accommodate the critical military training and service requirements of our assignments. We, on the other hand, were looking for opportunities to avoid trigonometry and Caesar. Anything would be better than these subjects, especially if we were assigned to the big guns. Besides, we were waiting for our chance to help turn the tide, after the many setbacks Germany had recently suffered. What was there really to being a soldier? It couldn't be much more than an extended camping period, something all of us had been through many times before. A little stricter maybe, but obeying a military command for a good purpose was better than having to bend constantly, at home, in school and in the Youth movement. Some of us just couldn't wait to go.

Jumping from the bus in front of the railroad station on the 12th, I spotted several of my classmates and their parents. They were speaking with a non-commissioned officer of the Luftwaffe. I soon learned it was Unteroffizier Schoenberger, who had been sent to meet us, and who would escort our group to his flak unit in the town of Kleutsch, near Dessau. He seemed like a regular guy, laughing at the quips some of the boys were making regarding their needs for sleep and rest, their big appetites, their desire for private rooms, plus many more inconsequential things that, in my opinion, mounted to no more than small talk. He told a few anecdotes of his own, drawing a few laughs from the parents and his captive audience. Looking at all our suitcases and baggage, his only comment was, "I predict that you will be sending most of your things home, once you are settled in."

Following our arrival in Dessau, we hiked the six kilometers to Kleutsch, a little farm village. As we walked through the settlement, we noticed farm buildings with their piles of manure, but also a few stores, and even a small school building. And right across the street from it, there were two dilapidated, one-story, wooden barracks structures. That was where we were heading. We couldn't believe our eyes. My impression was that refugees or prisoners must have occupied these buildings before we got here. The place looked shabby from the outside; no paint on the walls, just discolored wood. The windows were filthy, and there were even a few glass panes missing. The whole place was really drab. Our suitcases were waiting outside the buildings. Unteroffizier Schoenberger quickly ushered us into the barracks, telling us to be ready in fifteen minutes for another hike of two to three kilometers to the supply room in the battery area where we would eat, and be issued our uniforms and bedding. He didn't waste a minute blowing his whistle, which from here on would be our command to fall in.

When the last of us had picked up his issue, we headed back to Kleutsch, this time to put on our military gear and fix up a place to sleep, on our first night as a member of the Flak. The clothes I carried back with me fit alright; in fact, my HJ uniforms, i.e. the dress uniforms, were brand new, and so were the high shoes that went with that uniform. The work uniforms were strictly Luftwaffe issue. They were worn, but in fairly good shape, and they fit me fine. The helmet I was given was brand new and the right size; the gas mask fit also, with just minor adjustments to the straps. There was one piece of information we picked up from the supply room staff that was just delightful. We were told the HJ armband would not be worn with the military uniform. That was precisely what we were hoping for: to eliminate any signs connecting us with the Hitler Youth, now that we were soldiers. Next, we'd have to find ways to circumvent wearing the armband with our dress clothes, the HJ uniform. When I assessed my overall situation at that point, I considered myself fortunate that most of the things hastily thrown my way actually fit.

They got us up and out of the barracks at the crack of dawn the following morning, when the roosters crowed. Within minutes we were being hustled along to the main battery area, singing and double-timing until we were out of breath, huffing and puffing.

After our morning meal of milksoup, coffee, bread and a small hunk of butter, we were ushered into a conference room to meet

Oblt. Schrader, our battery commander, and receive a briefing on our mission and duties. We were being assigned to the 4./434 Heavy Flak Battery, a unit of eight stationary 88mm guns of the type proven in combat all over Europe, in Africa and in Russia. The *acht-acht* was a highly effective and reliable dual-purpose weapon, powerful, and capable of functioning as an antiaircraft and antitank gun.

We would be serving alongside regular troops of the Luftwaffe and Luftwaffenhelfer of an older age group who were assigned to the battery at an earlier date. While some of us would be assigned as gun crew members, others would be performing duties in the plotting room, on the range finder, or the listening apparatus. School attendance would be required first thing every weekday morning. Immediately following, we were to report for duty at our assigned stations in the main battery area. In the event of an alert while we were at school in Kleutsch, we would immediately leave the classroom and head for our assigned stations, on the double.

Because of our youth, we were entitled to a milk soup ration on the morning following any night alert. Each afternoon a period of time would be set aside for studying and homework.

We were advised considerable time would be spent on the subjects of gunnery, range finder operations, aircraft identification, and spotter duties, as well as equipment care and maintenance. We were also informed that we were here to replace the older group of Luftwaffenhelfer scheduled for release so they might be called up for regular military service. The mission of the battery, as we understood it, would be to defend the Junkers aircraft factory in Dessau from enemy air attack.

Following the orientation, we began a period of intensive training, since there was much to learn before we could function as fully competent crew members. We took it to heart; for us this was serious business, yet some of the NCOs just seemed to thrive on chicanery, on making life miserable for the "non-soldier soldiers," as they called us. Frequently, the daily routine included close order drill on the paved road, something we were good at. Looking to trip us up, the NCOs ordered us to double-time, first along the road, then into a grassed area, where we'd be ordered to hit the dirt and then immediately to get back on our feet. Still not

satisfied, the NCOs would direct our column—still at the double—
to change direction, right into a ploughed field where we would
again hit the ground several times, until halted and ordered to do
push-ups, and their famous "about face on the belt buckle." All
this in a field of dirt, often damp from an earlier shower. Our
appearance after such drills was disgusting, with dirt and mud
caked to our boots and uniforms.

But the harassment didn't end with the drill. On return to our
squad rooms, we might find that someone had been through our
wall lockers and with a flip of the wrist had emptied the shelves
onto the floor. "Lockers were messy," we were told. To compound
the agony, the contents of the lockers, which stood side by side,
were all mixed up; it took time to sort out our belongings from
those of the others in the room. On other occasions, the NCOs
called for a "masquarade party," requiring rapid changes into the
various uniforms we wore; from sports clothes to work suits to
dress uniforms and back, to start all over, again and again.

Our weekly clothing inspections were another way of getting
at us when we couldn't argue back. The breast pockets of our dress
uniforms were turned inside out, and the inspecting NCO scraped
along the inner seams with a toothpick until he came up with a bit
of lint. That was a violation, and the uniform was casually dropped
on the ground, where it would truly get dirty. The hobnails on the
bottom of our boots received the same toothpick treatment, and
there had better not be a single speck of dust in the crevices
between the sole and the hobnail, or a detail to scrub the outhouses
was a sure thing. Mercy upon him, too, who reported for inspection with a single hobnail missing from the sole of his boots.
Screams of negligence and disrespect for Luftwaffe property en-
sued, making the guilty one feel like a traitor. Private drill, in the
field, might be one of the methods used to punish such a culprit.
We took it; we had no choice. Gas mask drills were no different.
We'd march about in a teargas-filled room, and they'd order us to
take off our masks for prolonged periods of time. We were always
the underdogs.

It was understandable, then, when my friend Dieter took his
potato peels, and instead of throwing them in the garbage container, pulled a floorboard loose and threw the peels under the

barracks floor. We, his comrades, were aghast at first, but he didn't care much about health or sanitation, given our circumstances. The rest of us soon followed his example. One day I stuffed an oily rag into Schoenberger's drinking glass, which was standing in his open barracks window. When he found it, it seemed that doomsday had come. He called the boys in my group together and suggested that the guilty party step forward, or each and every one of us would share the guilt equally. Our situation was bad enough; I couldn't see the others having to suffer even more on my account. I stepped forward. He dressed me down and threatened to report me to the commanding officer, but in the end he let me off with just a personal warning; the only one I would ever receive. I was then sentenced on the spot to double-time around the newly built large barracks building in the main battery area, some fifty times. My ordeal lasted more than an hour; I was exhausted when it was over.

Despite the rough treatment we received from some of the military, we didn't care to spend our time in school, either. At break time, several of us would run to the *Gasthaus* up the street to inquire about the latest radio reports. By that time in the war, the location and direction of enemy bomber formations over the Reich was announced periodically on radio. As awful as the bombing raids were, we were always hoping for an alert that would get us out of the classroom and on our way to the gun emplacements, even if it meant running the entire distance from town, and then receiving a dressing-down for taking too long.

Eventually, the NCOs apparently felt we had been whipped into shape, for they became more friendly. They started to resemble human beings; human beings with authority, to be sure, but human beings nonetheless. We actually all started to get along pretty well. Following this informal upgrade in our status, I was assigned, along with several of my close friends, including Leithold and Moeser, to the plotting room crew. There, under the supervision of Obergefreiter Scholz, we posted the routes of approaching enemy aircraft, based on information transmitted to us either electrically or by earphone.

Some of the input we received came from the hearing apparatus located next to the Command Post. Whenever that crew would detect and zero in on an approaching target, the data would be passed to us, to be plotted on a large round board. In later months, a *Funkmessgeraet*, a radar, replaced the hearing apparatus we called the "big ears," as it had become obsolete. On sunny days, when the range finder crew could make visual sightings of the approaching enemy, the data developed electronically by their equipment would be relayed to the plotting room, where we would commence tracking the enemy's course and movements.

This experience, along with the theoretical gunnery training we were receiving, prepared those of us in the plotting room, to take on more responsible duties. First, we manned the spotter's scope on a rotating basis, looking for aircraft in the sky and making the proper identification. Later, Leithold and I were assigned to the range finder as members of the fire control crew; he as azimuth tracker, and I as elevation tracker. About that time, additional LH personnel assigned through the *Oberschule* in Schwarzenberg were added to the rolls of our battery; it was from this group that our replacements for the plotting room crew were drawn.

Being assigned to the fire control apparatus required us to participate twice daily in testing the lines and communications links between Command Post and guns, and Command Post and radar. Our routine equipment maintenance responsibilities included weekly treatment with talcum powder of all main cables running from the range finder to the gun positions. While we were busy doing these things, our classmates assigned to the guns were restocking and wiping down ammunition, and maintaining their gun tubes clean and ready for firing at a moment's notice. Theirs was bull work; handling ammunition and loading the guns could be back-breaking, especially during live action. Physically, our assignments at the Command Center were nowhere near as demanding. Still, we often joked that people with muscles were assigned to the gun crews, while only those with brains were allowed to serve on the range finder.

Night alerts and daytime alarm conditions were becoming a matter of routine. We were getting used to the daily run from the village; to being ready to fire for hours on end at night; and to scanning the skies for enemy intruders until our eyes hurt. It was especially hard to spot single planes. Generally, the lone flyers were British, most likely on reconnaissance missions in their light Mosquitos. Our battery opened fire whenever one of them came within range, but we were never fortunate enough to score a direct hit. They were built of plywood, we were told; a single hit would have knocked them right out of the sky. With the shells from our 88s bursting all around, they were lucky to get out of range in one piece, especially the ones that from time to time flew directly over our positions. Even at night, we could track them visually at the range finder if the moon lit up the sky sufficiently. It was a challenge to get a bearing on the elusive planes, as they dashed in and out of the clouds.

Even though the enemy thrust on its daytime runs was Leipzig to our south, Berlin to the north, or places like Magdeburg and Hannover, farther west, we were always in alarm condition, standing by our equipment, guns at the ready. Reports from intelligence told us that the Americans would approach in large formations, hundreds of them at a time, and then split into smaller groups to attack several targets in different locations simultaneously. Because of this strategy, we never knew where they would hit. On 28 May, close to 900 planes of the Eighth Air Force in fact made such a multiple-target attack. On that day, some 350 German fighters took to the skies to meet the enemy near Magdeburg. We were amazed at the number of fighters Field Marshal Goering had ordered out. With that many fighters up there, they would surely decimate the approaching bomber force. But it didn't work out that way.

The Americans went for eight primary targets, plus several others they decided on as the battle developed. We had no idea Dessau was on the list of the enemy's targets for the day. We fired many rounds; it was like giant fireworks. The thunder of our discharging guns, combined with the bursting sound of the projectiles the 88s were throwing up into the sky and the roaring of plane motors high above our heads, gave us a real feeling of being at war. In the distance, where Dessau is, and where we had observed a few target markers at first, there now hung a massive dark cloud, the sign of fire and destruction. Only thirty bombers were knocked out of the sky by the combined German forces of fighter planes and flak, a score we were not proud of.

The same thing happened all over again just two days later, on 30 May. Dessau, the city we were tasked to protect, was once again included on the Eighth Air Force target list. The battle raged fiercely, with our battery throwing hot shrapnel at the bomber formations high in the sky as fast as our men could fire and reload. The firing bell just kept ringing. The Junkers factory got it bad that time. Among the damage reports received, there was word that molasses was all over the street, several centimeters deep, next to the bombed plant where it was being made. Despite the agony and hurt just suffered by the people of Dessau, we joked about heading into town and gathering up a few buckets full of molasses so we'd have something to spread on our bread.

For our role in this battle, we were eventually awarded another ring to paint on our gun tubes and range finder, for downing one of the attackers.

On 6 June, the Allies invaded the coast of France in force and were able to gain a solid foothold on the beaches. We couldn't believe a landing would ever materialize, with the Atlantic Wall in place along the coast facing the British Isles; but very soon we learned differently. The news of the landings dwarfed the reports of the Russians' progress on the eastern front, and all our attention was focused on what was happening in Normandy.

The government offered a number of programs to students like ourselves. There was the *Wehrbauer* program, under which a volunteer would be given a farm in Poland, in return for working the land and concurrently serving as a "defense farmer," a type of uniformed militia, ready to take up arms around the clock. That had sounded enticing when it was first offered several years earlier, but by 1944 the appeal was wearing off, especially with the eastern front now moving in reverse direction, toward the Reich. An officer's candidate program, offered to students of higher learning institutions by the Wehrmacht, was much more appealing. Under this program, a candidate could be dismissed from school ahead of time, and exempted from completing the final graduation examination, provided his grades looked promising. Then, following a tour of duty on the front, the candidate would be rapidly promoted to the rank of lieutenant.

My folks had allowed me to express my interest in this program even before I was drafted. Now I was old enough, and received notice to report to Dresden for the formalization of the recruitment papers. Leave was granted by my flak unit for that purpose. I was surprised to find that only a handful of candidates were being processed while I was there.

Along with the other applicants, I was given a physical examination, and then a Wehrmacht colonel set up a number of physical group exercises, including boxing, climbing a high wall, and timed running. Each of the candidates was then interviewed by the senior officer, who sat at a desk in a large, drab and dimly lit office, with the candidate sitting on a chair in the center of the room. He asked me questions about the thirty-year war, and also about Kaiser Frederick the Great and the seven-year war of 1756–1763. I felt lucky, for I remembered the essential information from my history classes. Asked where I wanted to serve, I replied, "As a military attache in England."

"Why do you want to be assigned to England?" the officer asked me.

"I learned English in America; perhaps by serving in England after the war, I could help bring about peace and understanding."

"It is a little too soon for that, and it's too specialized. Right now we need front line officers; after a ninety-day tour in the field, you will know your capabilities better." The colonel stood up, ending the interview. I saluted, clicking my heels, did an about face, and left.

I wasn't sure how well I had made out until six weeks later, when I received my acceptance and a small silver pin signifying my status as an enrollee in the Officer's Candidate Program of the Wehrmacht.

More than 1,600 American bombers of the 8th and 15th Air Forces, escorted by in excess of 900 fighter planes, hit targets in central and southwest Germany on 20 July. This was an extremely large number of planes to be attacking in a single day. As usual, we were placed on alarm status when it became apparent that Leipzig, just sixty-five kilometers to our south, might be bombed. Days like this were exciting; we were forever busy, sorting out information on radar and visual sightings, trying to isolate enemy from friendly aircraft, and passing the information to the battery commander. However, this turned out to be a day of disaster.

We were not hit by the enemy, although that was always a possibility; instead, we were hit by grave news that made us ponder. Reports were received that an assassination attempt had been made on the Fuehrer at his headquarters near Rastenburg. He was alive, though injured. Plans by dissidents to disrupt the functioning of the government had also been foiled. We were dumbfounded; who would do a thing like this? How could it happen, with the elite of internal security all around Hitler? We could see the benefits of coming to terms with the Allies and going against the Soviets together, but even to think of assassinating the Fuehrer was preposterous in our opinion. We were to remain on alert even after the American and British air armadas returned to their bases. For us, this was to become a long day and night, and a time when each of us would assess, in his own way, what the future might bring.

Paris fell to the Allies during the latter part of August, while the Russians were making unprecedented advances, driving to the Vistula south of Warsaw and to the Baltic Sea near Riga. These things were happening about the same time plans were being formulated to transfer our battery to a new site in northwest Germany. Sitting in the hinterlands near Dessau was not the most efficient manner to employ the firepower of our eight guns.

Toward the end of the month, before preparations for the transfer got underway, the C.O. presented the Flak Activity Badge to one of the Youth members of the radar crew, and to me, for satisfactory services over a period of six months. Receiving the badge was an honor we had not expected, for only military personnel had been awarded the emblem before. We wore ours with pride.

Our Faehnrich, the officer's candidate assigned to our battery, received orders to act as advance party for the upcoming move. Word was passed that we would be getting things ready gradually, but that we would stay on line and ready for action until a few days before the guns would actually be pulled out from their permanent emplacements. Our particular guns were not wheel-mounted; they were designed for deployment as a stationary battery, with the guns bolted to heavy wooden platforms constructed inside earthen emplacements. As part of the advance preparations, our gun crews, assisted by a group of Russian volunteers, began to dig through the shoulder-high parapets of dirt that surrounded the 88s. Meanwhile, the advance detail traveled to Westfalia to inspect our new battery site and make initial arrangements with local authorities.

While the first V-2 rockets were hitting London, in early September, we were seriously preparing for our transfer to the vicinity of Minden, in Westfalia. There, we would be receiving four additional guns, giving the 4./434 a total of twelve tubes. In addition, we would be sharing a unified Command Post with an eight-gun battery, manned by Italians who were already in position. For us, this was an exciting change; now we would have real fire power. Just thinking of the damage our combined twenty guns could inflict, all firing at once, gave us renewed confidence in our power to make a difference.

The guns were among the first things to be moved. Crews were dispatched to a designated freight yard nearby, where the tubes and gunmounts were loaded onto open freight cars and readied for the long trip. Once the guns were shipped out, it was time to pack up the rest of the gear: the smaller pieces of equipment, cables, tools, and plotting and communications room items. Everything had to go, and everything going had to be packed. It was a busy period for us; we wanted to move faster, knowing we were out of commission and no longer on line, but everything had to be timed so the pieces would come together in the right sequence.

Most of us were given a short furlough to visit our homes before moving. However, train schedules and connections were miserable. Out in the country, enemy fighter planes were chasing the trains as they chugged along, knocking out the locomotives as soon as they showed themselves. Unwanted layovers became a regular routine, but any delays had to be certified on the travel documents by the military travel authorities or the field gendarmes. Having to justify one's delays was an unpleasant experience, since the authorities expected the traveler to leave home earlier, knowing that delays should be expected. My trip home netted a reprimand for me on my return for failing to have my orders stamped. What Oblt. Schrader did not know was that I purposefully left home late, anticipating a delay along the way that did not materialize. My heart was pounding when I reported my late arrival, knowing I had done wrong. He probably guessed it, but didn't pursue the matter. The dressing-down I received was as bad as facing a firing squad, though, and I knew I'd never be late again.

Finally, in mid-October, the men of the 4./434 were ready to move out. When all of the battery's equipment, supplies and also our personal belongings had been loaded on the freight train, we crawled into the cattle car reserved for the troops. A good measure of straw covered the entire floor of the wagon, and it was not too difficult to pick a spot to call your own for the duration of the trip. We slept well, despite the discomforts of the bumpy ride. Stops were made along the way every now and then, allowing us to fill our canteens and perhaps pick up the latest news from one of the local people. We, too, experienced being strafed by a low-flying plane; it swooped down on us out of nowhere while the train was stopped at a small station. Luckily most of us were outside stretching our legs; that allowed us to dash under the train, and the cover of the cars. The pilot made only one pass and kept going; we cursed him, but were inwardly thankful he didn't decide to come back for another run.

It was dark when we arrived in the area of the main station in Minden, during the latter part of October. Our Faehnrich was standing near the tracks in the freightyard, waiting. On clearing the box car, we brushed off our uniforms quickly, and set out for another part of the city. From there a narrow gage train would take us to our final destination, a village called Stemmer. Because of the darkness, we were allowed to move along sidewalks instead of marching in the streets as we normally would.

Suddenly, sirens began to howl warnings of imminent danger; within minutes, bombs were falling. We heard the whistling and whizzing of falling bombs not too far off, and we were ordered to take cover. The explosions shook the ground we were on, and human instinct made us hug the pavement even harder. The all clear was not too long in coming, however, and we continued on our way to the train.

We had never seen or experienced a narrow gage railroad. The cars were small and narrow, almost dainty, like oversized toys. The engine was chugging along so slowly that one of the boys yelled out, for everyone to hear, "Picking flowers while the train is in motion is verboten." That gave us our first laugh since arriving in Minden. Looking out the car windows, we could easily envision jumping off the train, picking a flower or two, and hopping back on, without any difficulty. This struck us as really funny. Now that the ice of seriousness had been broken, there were more jokes, and we laughed the rest of the way.

From the station in Stemmer we marched to the school building, where we were going to be billeted temporarily. Several classrooms had been emptied out and straw was brought in for us to sleep on. This set-up seemed informal enough. We liked it. Sleeping in our uniforms that first night didn't really matter; at least we would be getting a good night's sleep. There were no guns to man this night.

The next morning we were fed from a field kitchen set up across the street from the school, next to a grocery store bearing my family name. That drew a few jokes and comments from my classmates; they were spreading the word that I could get anything from the proprietor, without ration cards and money. We had a few laughs, but the seriousness of the times soon caught up with us again. We were told we would be digging the guns in and erecting prefab structures nearby so we could be billeted on site. That seemed like back-breaking work; twelve guns, barracks for more than a hundred troops, and special places for the C.O. and the NCOs. Now we would be performing the duties of the *Arbeitsdienst*, shoveling dirt every day, for weeks on end. Marching to the battery site near the settlement of Holzhausen II/Brede each morning, we glanced at our big 88s, which were being temporarily stored inside a barn in Stemmer. Knowing we were working and sweating to bring these guns on line made us feel that the heavy work and muscle aches were well worth it.

Time flew by as we progressed with the work. Winter was upon us, and it was getting cold. With the ground beginning to freeze, we now had to resort to the use of picks as well as spades and shovels. The regular Luftwaffe soldiers, our Russian volunteers and a contingent of men from another unit did most of the bull work. They were moving the extremely heavy beams for the gun platforms into place, and bolting them together, while we were working on the parapets. Hearing of the massive counteroffensive that Field Marshal Rundstedt had launched in the Ardennes gave us a boost to speed up our work.

Our guns were in place by Christmas, although it would take more time to bring them on line. Now, we also had to work on the new barracks. The back-and-forth between Stemmer and the new battery site would have to end soon, especially if we were to be back in a ready status before too long. At present, formations of Fortresses and Liberators were carrying death and destruction deep into the Reich without being challenged by our battery; and we were directly in their flight path to Brunswick, Hannover and Berlin. The Italians in the fields just beyond our site were on alert every day, without exception; we were anxious to join them, to get our combined units operating as a Super Battery.

Oblt. Schrader arranged a Christmas Party for the entire battery in a *Gasthaus* in Friedewalde, about three kilometers from Stemmer, shortly before the holiday. We enjoyed the opportunity to speak and mingle, giving us a chance to meet some of the members in our battery whom we otherwise would never get to know. Busy as we always were, we had never fully realized we had a few Flakhelferinnen in our unit, girls serving in our communications room. There was a pretty one among them, and I took an immediate liking to her. But she remained aloof; we were just boys, she told me. Sure, I thought, they wanted men—the NCOs maybe. I didn't let it bother me, but I was disappointed at being rebuffed.

On New Year's Eve I was guarding the guns in the new emplacements. This was a lonely duty; walking around out there, all alone, and without a weapon, watching twelve of Germany's treasured and most feared artillery pieces. We could not be issued individual weapons because of our status and age, even though foreign workers were known to be committing acts of sabotage in the area. There was nothing to prevent us from carrying a concealed weapon, however, as long as it was not a firing arm. For these reasons I had brought an S.A. dagger back with me the last time I'd gone home on furlough. On this night, I slipped it into the side of my jack boots. I felt a little better knowing I could protect myself if I had to, but I also knew I could be jumped out there,—all by myself, and no one would ever know it. So I did my job—I walked between the emplacements, stopped, listened, looked around, walked some more, and never in a regular pattern—but I only peeked at the inside of the emplacements from the parapet entrances. There were just too many nooks and crannies, plus the dug-outs in there; I felt uncomfortable and insecure about going in alone and without a flashlight.

Shortly before midnight I heard footsteps; they were deliberate, and coming from the direction of Stemmer. I positioned myself so I could observe the approaching figure; it was one of our boys. I let out a sigh of relief and wished him luck, then headed back to the schoolhouse in Stemmer. The New Year had just been rung in, and one of the regulars from the range finder crew offered me a stiff drink as I walked through the door, telling me to warm up on this cold night. It had been cold and unappealing in more than one way, I thought; I downed the glass of schnapps in a single gulp. I coughed, my insides burning; I had never had any of this stuff in all my life. But I warmed up quickly, while those standing about were laughing, and wishing me a happy New Year.

Most of the billeting units we erected were small, four-man Finnish huts, oblong in shape and made of a composite or pressed board. The siding material was just like the round huts the Russian volunteers were occupying. To provide for maximum protection, we first dug the ground out about two meters deep, and then erected the prefabricated building. The excess dirt was then piled up above ground on all sides of the sunken building. When our hut was finished, we agreed that we had a fairly secure place in which to live and sleep. Straw was piled almost a meter high into the back half of the small structure, and held steady by boards we nailed in place. That section became our sleeping area; we divided it up equally. The front half was the living area. My friend Leithold nailed a few boards together to make a table with a shelf underneath, so he would have a place to stack his clothes. Moeser and the rest of us rigged up whatever we needed to make the place more liveable.

Among the things I had picked up at home on my last trip was a metal first aid kit from the Boy Scouts of America. I had originally brought it with me when we first came to Germany back in 1937. We never had any use for the kit at home, but I thought it might come in handy around here, so I hung the container on the wall above Leithold's table. During a subsequent inspection I was asked what "that box" was, and explained it contained first aid materials. Nothing more was said; the box stayed on the wall, and luckily, never had to be used here, either.

We lived on site starting in early January 1945, but our school classes (the few we were attending, now that we were on alert most of the time) were held in Stemmer, about one and a half kilometers away. That meant marching to school from our field installation each morning, and back at noon, although we usually ended up double-timing back around 10:00 or 10:30 in the morning because of alert conditions. The fields all around us were of pure, rich and dark humus, and good and soft after the spring thaw. After a rain, we'd be in mud up to our ankles, dragging the muck into our hut, getting our clothes dirty, ruining our boots and shoes. The wooden pegs used by the cobbler were rotting out; we were in a real mess. Footprints in the mud became puddles to be avoided, and the entire area near the billets and the range finder was a catastrophe. Similar conditions prevailed in the gun sections, further up the dirt path.

Frohberger, a schoolmate of mine, asked one Sunday if I wanted to go to Minden with him to get some wooden shoes, the type the Dutch wear. That sounded good; the NCOs had already acquired leather boots for themselves with wooden soles, and some were walking around with Dutch clogs on their feet. One of Frohberger's friends joined us, and we headed for the city. He knew just where to go: the freight yard. I was confused, why the freight yard? "That's where the clogs are," Frohberger explained. "We'll go get them, and you stand watch. Call us if anyone comes," and they jumped the fence. There on the track stood an open rail car, filled to the very top with wooden shoes. I had never seen actual wooden clogs, and to see a whole railcar full of them was almost unreal, but there they were. My friends were fast; within minutes they were back and we hightailed it out of there. I hadn't realized they were planning to steal the clogs; I thought Frohberger knew of a place where we could buy them. Oh well, I thought, too late to think about it now. We caught the next train back, keeping the clogs under our greatcoats until we got back to our huts and could try them on. They wore well. The trip had been worth it. Every now and then one of the clogs would get stuck in the mud, but we knew nothing would ever be perfect.

During this time we received our promotion to Luftwaffenoberhelfer, the rank of senior auxiliarists. This entitled us to wear a silver stripe on our epaulets. Since the designation was given out across the board after twelve months of service, all of us suddenly became "seniors"; there were no subordinates. Still, it made us feel good to wear the silver stripe; we had earned it with our aching muscles and sweat. More so than ever before, we were now up and on alert every night. During the day there was a constant stream of American air armadas flying over us with their fighter escorts. Thundering motors, bellowing guns, and the dull sounds of bursting projectiles high in the sky were the norm. If there were none, we considered it a dull day. Every now and then, bold fighter pilots would hedgehop through the country side and whiz by our emplacements, so close we could see the men in the cockpits of their planes. There was never enough time to train a gun on them, not even the 20mm weapon assigned to us at that time. Some of the men would be lucky to get a few rifle shots off, but they weren't able to bring a plane down. We could see the pilots looking at us as they were flying by; we thought we saw them grinning. Maybe they were; they had one up on us.

Our attitude toward the Allies, whom we had set high above the Soviets until now, changed abruptly as a result of the vicious and ruthless bomb and incendiary attacks on Dresden during the night of 13 February, and again during the following two days. Dresden was a cultural metropolis of 650,000 residents, bulging with many more thousands of refugees fleeing the advancing Soviet forces. British Lancaster bombers hit the city twice in one night. They came in two waves that night, just three hours apart, a total of 1,400 planes, at first dropping high explosives and following up with in excess of a half million incendiaries. It was a holocaust, a well planned firestorm that killed some 100,000 civilians and left many more homeless. The resultant tornado hurled these innocent people, civilians and children, into the man-made fires of hell, while others suffocated from lack of oxygen. The next day, the Americans came with an armada of many hundreds of their Flying Fortresses to add further shame to the misery below. Allied planes had been branded "terror bombers" many times before; the Dresden raids confirmed it. We had previously been inclined to consider the pictures of captured flying jackets brandishing the words "Murder, Inc." as mere propaganda, but now we knew better.

As the weather began to improve, we were busy outside, working on the parapets around the combined Command Post and the radar. Reeds were brought in by the truckload, so we could reinforce the dirt walls around the range finder and the walkway through the parapet that surrounded our fire control equipment. The men in the gun section were doing similar work in their respective emplacements. Once that was completed, we commenced digging individual fox holes for ourselves, outside the Command Post. Just before noon, on 28 March, Minden was again attacked. It was the fifth or sixth time since the beginning of the war. Our guns kept blasting away, round after round; the firing bell got a real workout, calling for a salvo from each of our 12 tubes every three seconds. When it was over, the inner city had been reduced to rubble and 171 civilians had lost their lives. This brought Minden's air war death toll to 412.

As of 1 April, Easter Sunday, the Soviets had secured Pomerania and crossed the Oder River; Allied airborne units had landed behind German lines at Wesel, the Rhine had been crossed, and American ground units were driving deep wedges into the heart of Germany. The discouraging news notwithstanding, the people of Stemmer invited some of the Luftwaffenhelfer boys to their homes for Easter dinner and a period of relaxation. Those accepting the invitations spent pleasant and memorable hours with host families who wanted to make them feel welcome, wanted and cared about. Several of us spent the afternoon with a family and their two daughters and had an enjoyable time. The family liked us and asked that we return the following Sunday, 8 April. We were overjoyed; finally somewhere to go, something to do, someone to talk with. "Yes, thank you," we said, "We'll be back." So we thought.

For us, 8 April in Stemmer would never come. It was on 4 April that the people of Stemmer heard our guns for the last time.

———————————————————— 7

Becoming American

Wintering over at POW Camp 2228 from 1945 to 1946, with the rain and sleet, the icy winds, and the drifting snow from inside our flimsy tents, for months on end, was enough for me to finally want to make one of the homeward-bound shipments of prisoners. I had been hoping to put off the trip into the Russian Zone for as long as possible, but it was inevitable. I was suffering from a bad case of insecurity regarding my future. All we knew of the Russians was from the days when they were fighting their way into Germany, letting out their hatred, and mercilessly killing anyone who got in their way. We had heard plenty during the war about their Secret Police, and the commissars who shot their own men without much provocation. These things kept sticking in my mind, and I was not alone with these thoughts.

During the spring thaw, however, my fear of the Russians began to be tempered by a mounting feeling of desperation, as I made my way back and forth through the everlasting mud flats that persisted despite the few walkways we had built. The camp was dismal. When our compound was emptied once more and we were told that new arrivals were not expected for several weeks, I was asked to help out in Compound 18, across the street, since their interpreter had been sent home with the last batch of returnees. It wasn't too bad, going over there every morning and returning late in the afternoon; it amounted to going on a work detail. That arrangement lasted but a short time, when the British decided a permanent transfer to Compound 18 would be more appropriate; that way I could stay there, without going through the daily sign-in and sign-out routine. Then I had to admit that I had been pretty fortunate being on the staff of Compound 5 and having my own tent, and even a bunk. In 18, I learned how the others had been living, sleeping on the bare ground with nothing but a poncho or shelter half between the dirt and their bodies. The tent I was assigned to had not been winterized; I suppose it hadn't been used for sleeping.

During this unwelcome assignment I often caught myself standing at the gate, looking through the barbed wire at Compound 5 across the street, which was still occupied only by a few staff members, all people I knew. I was longing to get back over there. I knew that place like the back of my hand; was as if I'd grown up there; and our lighthouse at the gate looked mighty nice, too. Luckily, the same NCO of the British Provost Guard remained at Compound 5, even after my transfer. I did get a chance every now and then to speak with him. He was friendly, always asked how I was. One day I gave in to my false pride and told him I was miserable and wanted to get back across the street. He smiled, saying, "Don't worry, *Dolmetscher,* we are expecting a new bunch of prisoners in a few days; we'll bring you back over here then." That was the boost I needed, and I fared well a little longer.

The one good thing that happened in the course of the year was being allowed to send out POW letters with short messages, to which I was beginning to receive answers. I heard from my mother; she and my little sister Annerose were fine, but they had not received any word from my dad who was last known to be in East Prussia. A letter I received from my grandfather in New York contained an address for Aunt Edith, who was now in Frankfurt. I couldn't understand how she managed to get there; last I knew, she was living with us in what was now the Russian Zone. I felt good about having reestablished contact with my family in both Germany and America, and I kept in touch the best I could.

In mid-May 1946 it was my turn to head back to Germany, again in a cattle car loaded with prisoners. Crossing the Rhein brought tears to our eyes, especially when someone started singing, "Oh, Du wunderschoener deutscher Rhein," and we all chimed in. Later, as the train passed through the stations closer to Munsterlager, our destination in the Lueneburger Heath, we saw women lining the platforms, holding up pictures of soldiers and asking if we recognized their loved ones, of whom they still had no information a year after the war. Being in Munsterlager was a relief; at least we were on German soil once again. The men hailing from areas farther east were now also much closer to their homes located in the dreaded Russian Zone of Occupation. There was an air of uneasiness when the POWs living in the Western Zones were promptly discharged while the rest of us were kept waiting. But then those of us without visible afflictions were notified we were being shipped to England to bring in the harvest. I was overjoyed; this would give me more time to think and plan, and maybe hear better news of home. On the other hand, though, we were beginning to suspect we might be destined to become permanent prisoners of whatever power had us in their custody.

Within days of the good news, we were back in boxcars as usual, heading for the coast and a ship, waiting to take us across the North Sea to England. It was a thrill getting on the boat and being able to walk around freely to enjoy the fresh sea breeze. The ship was immaculate; a troop transport, well maintained by the British. For the first time I could see with my own eyes the graveyards of German ships, just as we were heading out to sea and into deeper water. Many of the ships that went down were sitting on the bottom, upright, with only the tops of their masts showing. The crosses were silent reminders of the ugliness and rewards of war.

I soon struck up a conversation with one of the English crew members who was winding up a line. He amazed me to no end when he said the Germans had been in the wrong alliance. I didn't understand, so he explained: the British with their diplomatic expertise and know-how, combined with the Germans and their military knowledge, could have licked the United States. I couldn't believe what I was hearing. Was there discontent among the Allies? How profound was it? I asked him why he felt this way; I was curious, but also, mistrusting anyone I spoke with, I wanted to be sure he wasn't just setting me up to be turned in. He merely said, the Americans are too boisterous, have lots of money and throw their weight around too much; he had no liking for them, but also bore no animosity towards the Germans. These were words I would expect from a die-hard Nazi, not from a young sailor fortunate enough to have been on the winning side. When he moved along, continuing his assigned chores, I sat for a while, staring across the water, silent and withdrawn.

Soon after docking in England, we were ushered into comfortable passenger cars, a new twist to POW rail transportation. Certainly it was a 100 percent improvement over the manner in which we were shuttled around in the war zones. For about a week or two, I was among transients, being routed to some unknown destination via a series of camps, all of which were superb compared to the facilities I had seen on the mainland. The British were reasonable and fair with us. The prisoners were still bartering their rings and watches for cigarettes and tobacco from the guards. It was apparent that some of the prisoners had held on to their treasures all this time; perhaps some would actually bring their sentimental belongings back home with them.

On my travels, I met and hung around with a few young fellows my own age. I surprised myself at how fast I was making new friends, when not too long ago, I thought the world would come to an end when my classmates were shipping out and I stayed behind. I was finally assigned to Camp 250, Thorpe Hall, near Bridlington, where we worked helping local farmers bring in the harvest. The farmer spoke with me often, always conversing in his language. On one of these occasions he asked a few questions about my American background, and finally said he would let one of the officers know of me.

After clearing the field of flax, and harvesting various other crops over the next week or two, I was detailed to repairing metal and wooden folding benches. One day while making the repairs, I observed a motorcycle driving up. An officer dismounted; he was a major, who briefly spoke with the supervising civilian. Both were looking my way. Then the officer approached me. "Soldier, are you the American?" he wanted to know.

"Yes, sir—that is, I was born in America." I really didn't know the right answer to his question; I had heard so much talk about my origins lately that I was more confused than ever.

"What are you doing here, if you are an American?" he asked. This required some explanation, so I gave him a quick rundown on the circumstances surrounding my presence in his camp. When I finished, he said, "I believe that having been born in America, and being a minor, you might rightfully be an American. I am going to London very soon and I will speak with someone at the American Embassy. Meanwhile, you file an application for discharge, giving the facts as you just explained them to me. Well, cheerio, and carry on." He turned about, hopped on his motorcycle and drove off.

It was hard for me to believe that I should really be an American. My father is German, and so is my mother, and we live in Germany. Might I be the only American in the family because of being born in Pawtucket? The thought of such a possibility was certainly appealing. But I wasn't going to file an application; not just yet. What if the Embassy said I was American, and they decided to send me right back to America with no questions asked? I couldn't just walk out on my folks, stuck in the Russian Zone; especially when there was no news of my father's whereabouts. What if the Americans didn't understand or recognize the circumstances under which I was drafted? The major had left me with much to think about.

Thorpe Hall was one of several smaller camps under the umbrella of Camp 250. We were being housed in nisson huts made of corrugated steel that gave the appearance of semicircular arches in cross-section. Each of us was assigned a bunk with a mattress. Our billets were much like those of the British regulars. Camp 250 supplied us with laundry soap and other essentials, such as clothing and shoes. The food was fit for the best; we had no complaints.

One night after work, I was notified to get my things together in a hurry, as I was being transferred. A guard picked me up, and we travelled by courier vehicle to Camp 81, near Brigg. On our arrival, a German NCO of the camp staff was standing near the gate with a weird grin on his face, "What do we have here, another one for Detention Camp?" My British escort shook his head.

During the checking-in process, I learned I was being sent to London. Proceedings were rapid. Early the next morning I left again with a personal escort. We traveled together in regular passenger cars, sitting side by side, this time intermingled with civilians who were taking the same train. For most of the trip we were chatting in a relaxed atmosphere, and time went by fast.

In London we were met by Military Police and taken to a mansion in Kensington Palace Gardens, near Hyde Park. It was the London District Cage, seat of the British War Crimes Investigations Unit. From the outside, this was just another well-guarded building with a barbed wire fence around it. Throwing my small duffel bag over my shoulders, I entered the building, stopping at the check-in desk. I couldn't help but notice the wide set of stairs with the solid banisters leading to the next floor a few meters away. Just then, a loud voice from above announced, "Prisoner coming down!" The guard behind the desk jumped up, ordering me to drop my bag and turn around. I was puzzled, but did as I was told. I asked why I had to turn around so suddenly, and the guard explained that the prisoners were not to see one another. I wondered why.

My escort, meanwhile, dropped off an envelope he was carrying, wished me well, and left. The soldier at the desk asked, "What did you do, or what do you know?"

I didn't know how to reply, except to say, "Maybe I'm here because I was born in America."

He then searched my person and belongings, taking away the papers and pictures I was carrying on me; I objected, but got nowhere with him. After stuffing my things back into the duffel bag, another guard escorted me up the stairs, first calling to the guard on the next landing, "Prisoner coming up!" On the second floor, he opened one of the doors and motioned for me to go through. Four middle-aged men, well-groomed and dressed in snappy German uniforms, were standing in the room, talking. They discontinued their conversation when I entered, looking in my direction. I had the impression they were people with authority; they just looked like officers. I felt awkward, like a spotlight was shining on me.

"Gentlemen, I am Luftwaffenhelfer Schröder," I said by way of introduction.

The tallest one in the group, a grey-haired man with a friendly smile, approached me with his right hand extended, saying, "Well, here we are, all together, from the little antiaircraft auxiliarist, to the top general of the elite. I am Oberstgruppenfuehrer Wolff." He was a top Waffen SS officer, with the rank of Generaloberst. I shook his hand. He continued, "And next to me are Generals Felmy, Luftwaffe; General of the Infantry, Gareis; and over there, at the window, a colonel from Austria."

I responded routinely, "Guten Tag; es freut mich Ihre Bekanntschaft zu machen," pleased to meet you. At this point, I had no idea what we were all doing here.

There was an empty cot near the door, which Wolff said I could use. He explained to me that he had been transferred from Nuremberg after extensive interrogations by the Americans, arriving in London just days before me. When I had settled, he resumed telling his story to the others; it was fascinating. Wolff had been very close to Hitler and Himmler. He served as the highest ranking SS officer in Italy, where he acted as a diplomat to the Italians and the Vatican. He was Himmler's personal representative to Wehrmacht and other German forces in that country, and also the principal SS and Police officer. Amazingly he had secretly conferred with American OSS and military personnel on Swiss soil, offering to orchestrate the surrender of all German forces in Italy, including troops in the western part of Austria, notwithstanding Hitler's orders to the contrary. These clandestine negotiations supposedly resulted in the surrender of one million men, and the collapse of Germany's southern front on 2 May.

As fantastic as his story sounded, and as appropriate as his actions seemed under the circumstances, I could not believe an officer of his rank and position would violate the trust placed in him by his superiors; in his case, by Hitler himself. I had to reason, however, that his actions saved many lives for Germany as well as the Allies; in the final analysis, that took precedence over any pledge of loyalty or obedience. Besides, if some of the highest ranking officers in the hierarchy had chosen disloyalty over a fight to the death as advocated by the Fuehrer, then they must have had good reasons that we may not have known about. As I struggled to better understand, a feeling of having been deceived and cheated by National Socialism came over me. Inwardly, I was angered.

General der Flieger, Helmut Felmy, reminded me of the elderly reserve major we had as a teacher while in Kleutsch; he seemed old and tired. I learned he had been in command of German forces in southern Greece from 1941–1942 and, commencing in 1943, commanding general of an army corps. The other general in the room, Martin Gareis, of the Infantry, had a pleasant personality. He was about fifty-five and had commanded the 89th Division, made up primarily of men from the *Sudetenland.* Toward the end of the war he commanded the 46th Panzer Corps. The Austrian Colonel kept to himself most of the time. Even though Austria and Germany had become a single entity in 1938, there appeared a sudden animosity among prisoners, with the Austrians disclaiming any allegiance to Germany or responsibility for the war. As a result, Germans snubbed the Austrians, and this may have been the reason the Colonel's name was not mentioned to me during Wolff's introduction of his roommates.

Next morning, I was called out and taken to the ground floor where a British officer was waiting for me. I walked up to his desk, planted my feet solidly on the ground and stood at attention, until told to be at ease. The officer asked a number of questions about myself, then switched to making statements he wanted me to supplement or confirm. "You were nine when you were taken to Germany? You were drafted right from school at age fifteen? When was the last time you heard from your father; what was his job, and where is he now?" He asked a number of other questions on matters he just could not have known about without completing an investigation on me and my family. I was somewhat ill at ease; he knew too much, and being in England, that was a bit out of the ordinary. I cooperated fully and answered all the questions to the best of my knowledge. I surmised he already knew whatever he was fishing for, so why hide anything; besides, what was there to hide in the first place?

I returned to my room when it was over. During my absence, the officers had been called out for their daily one-hour walk in the yard of the mansion. The guard assigned to our floor came into the room with one finger across his lips, pointing to several places on the ceiling where I could see slight discolorations in the whitewash. I stood there silently, and followed him out of the room when he waved for me to come. Outside, he said, "Everything you say in there can be overheard. The people in your room are a bad influence on you, so I'd suggest you volunteer to work in the kitchen and stay out of there as much as you can."

I was surprised at receiving the warning and certainly had no objection to spending my time in the kitchen area, where I was kept busy washing and scrubbing pots and pans most of the time. While working, I found out that war criminals as well as prosecution witnesses were being processed at the Cage before being sent to the mainland for the trials. Along with the larger Nuremberg war crimes tribunal, a number of smaller proceedings were underway throughout Europe, mostly in areas once occupied by German forces. How I ever got here, I didn't know; perhaps this was the only place where they could decide on the disposition of my case. I was sure that time would tell.

The next time I saw the floor guard, he whispered he had heard I would be sent back to America. My reaction may have been a bit abrupt. "America, I don't want to go to America. My family is in Germany. I need to find out how they are, first."

"Well, they'll probably send you to Germany first, anyway, and from there to America," he reassured me.

A few days later, Generals Felmy and Gareis and I were notified to prepare for a flight to Germany. That was easy for me, since all I had was a duffel bag. Felmy had a problem; he owned several suitcases and trunks, plus a number of other cumbersome pieces that would also have to go. Though we were promptly moved to transient quarters, our departure was delayed, "because General Felmy has too much baggage." Within days, we were on our way aboard a troop ship sailing for Germany.

On this trip, I received another surprise. Our officers, even though prisoners of war, were to dine in the officer's mess aboard ship. And, to maintain proper etiquette and protocol, they were to be served their meals by lower ranking German personnel. Several other officers had joined our group at the time of sailing, but only one additional enlisted person was included besides myself. This meant I would be waiting at the German officer's table. By now, my head had been filled with ideas of being an American, and being on my way back to America, so why should I be waiting on the German generals? I reasoned, however, that the short trip from England would entail no more than one or two meals anyway, and I resolved not to make a fuss about such a triviality.

One of the British soldiers accompanying our group on the cross-channel trip, became my personal escort following our landing and disembarkation in Germany. Stopping at a checkpoint, the Military Police officer on duty told me to empty my duffel bag onto a ground cloth in front of him. As he was poking through my sad collection of belongings with his night stick, flipping individual pieces of clothing around, my escort cautioned, "Go easy, his mother is an American." The MP looked up at me and apologized, telling me to pack up and move along. I knew my escort had the story wrong, but what did it matter; we were on our way once more. That my "American connection" was being respected provided me with a renewed sense of confidence.

We took the night train to Frankfurt, riding in a compartment specially set aside for the two of us. It was a relaxing journey; we talked about the war and what was happening now that it was over. My escort left the compartment for a moment, and when he returned, he told me there was an American next door, interested in meeting me. I didn't waste a second, jumping up after receiving the nod to leave, and racing out the door. I knocked at the compartment door next to ours and was welcomed by a young man wearing an American uniform that resembled that of an officer, but wasn't. Smiling, he invited me to sit down. He was an American, alright; his English sounded different than what I had been hearing for the past sixteen months, and he also seemed more casual than most of the British I had met during that period. I was beaming at the opportunity to meet this American face to face. He was the first American I'd seen in over nine years.

He told me he was a civilian, working for the military government, and he explained that most of the likewise employed American civilians were wearing similar uniforms with appropriate insignia. Being involved in German affairs professionally, he showed a great interest in my background. He thought I'd make out alright once I got back home. He meant I would do alright after being discharged in the American Zone, now that I had changed my residence to an address in Frankfurt which Aunt Edith had supplied in one of her letters. For hours we talked and snacked, and drank Coca Cola. How refreshing it was. I had not felt that sparkly feeling running down my throat in all the years I lived in Germany. The closest I ever came to Coca Cola was seeing it advertised before the war on a sign nailed to the fence outside the rifle club in my home town, but we never went inside to buy any.

When I finally left the American's compartment just after midnight, he handed me a few packs of cigarettes and gum, and wished me well. My escort was sitting up in our compartment, reading, when I reported back. He seemed pleased that I enjoyed my visit with the American. I immediately settled back to catch a few relaxing hours of sleep, never once feeling or hearing the train's bumpy and noisy ride.

Standing inside the Frankfurt terminal the next morning, waiting for our pick-up, we watched a group of young uniformed Americans who had also just arrived. Their heads were shaven like prisoners, but they were soldiers, maybe recruits. We could not have missed them, for they were loud and boisterous, laughing and joking, and swearing profusely. My British escort looked at me, and I at him. We both smiled, but said nothing. I was disappointed in the behavior of this group, but I admired the many other American soldiers milling around the station. They were smartly dressed, with sharp creases in their trousers, looking sporty with their short jackets. Their pointed caps, pushed one side or forward close to their brows, made them look cocky but confident; they seemed sure of themselves and of their purpose for being here. Oh, how I wished I could become one of them.

An American MP van pulled up in front of the station to take us on our journey to Oberursel, the Military Intelligence Center for the European Theater, where my escort bade me farewell and I was ushered into a cell with a single bed. An MP told me to remove my shoelaces and leave them with him. "Why do you want my shoelaces?"

"Orders!" he replied.

"If you are afraid I might hang myself, what about the rope in my duffel bag?" He replied he had no orders to search the duffel bag. I couldn't quite understand the Americans' reasoning. But then, there were so many things I did not understand.

My cell was roomy enough. It had a solid door with a small window in it, so the guard in the corridor could see what was going on inside. Restroom facilities were outside the cell off the main hall. Soon after my arrival I asked to use the facilities. The guard opened the door and jumped back quickly, with his hand ready on his holstered nightstick. "Don't worry, I ain't gonna make a run for it," I assured him, butchering my English so he'd be sure to recognize it as American.

He pointed to the door of the restroom. On my return, he asked, "Are you a Yank?"

"I was born in the States, but got stuck out here. Right now, I don't know what nationality I'm supposed to be," I said as the lock clicked behind me.

My cell had a barred window to the outside world that could be opened to let fresh air in. Looking out, I could see another wing of the building immediately to my right. It, too, was lined with barred windows. As I was gazing out into nowhere, contemplating my future, I couldn't help but think of the many Allied fliers that had been in these same cells not too long ago, when the place was still an interrogation center for the Luftwaffe, known as Dulag Luft.

The next day, following a short interrogation, I was taken to Marburg for demobilization and discharge at Disarmed Enemy Forces Enclosure 15. Once again I was a loner, a special prisoner. A few hours after arriving, a call went out for "the American" to report to the discharge desk. Everyone stared at me as I headed for the discharge center. They were probably wondering what an American was doing among them, while I was wondering what prompted the camp staff to refer to me as "the American" when I was really a POW, a nobody. The interviewer made one final check of the "wanted list," a thick volume sitting on his desk, before I was cleared and handed my discharge papers and a voucher for a train ticket to Frankfurt. I received no discharge money, since I had not been a prisoner of the Americans, only a transient. At least, that's how my discharge read.

A German driver took me to the Marburg railroad station in a U.S. Army truck and dropped me off. From there, I could catch a train to Frankfurt. Oh, how good it felt to be free, to be standing alone in the train station, without an armed escort for the first time in seventeen months. Still, I felt awkward, even timid, when I tried walking up to the counter to ask for train information and to trade my voucher for a ticket. It seemed a thousand spotlights were aimed at me, making me hot and sweaty. I couldn't understand why I felt that way, in my time of happiness; I should have been laughing out loud, but I couldn't. The agent hardly looked at me when he handed me the ticket, no questions asked.

I looked the ticket over very closely, making sure it was correct. Although there had not been any mustering-out pay for me, I'd been given enough cash to provide me with food and lodgings in Frankfurt for three days. That meant I'd have to find work and a place to live very quickly; three days wasn't very much. Still, it was better than nothing. There were less fortunate people—millions were still homeless and unemployed. At least as a POW I was being fed and housed, while others were struggling for bare survival. Assessing my current situation realistically, I had to admit I hadn't suffered any physical hardships that I couldn't handle. I could dismiss them all as misfortunes or inconveniences brought about by the circumstances of the times.

Sitting on a bench in the waiting room, I opened the envelope with my discharge papers to look them over, now that I could settle down in peace and quiet until the train arrived. It was a great feeling, holding the paper that said I was free and no longer a prisoner of war. It took a little time to fully comprehend the reality of my changed status. There were other documents in the envelope, including my transfer to London, and also a handwritten communication that my aunt Melanie, of Providence, Rhode Island, had written to the British camp commandant. After reading her lines, it became clear to me for the first time where the interrogating officer at London District Cage had picked up the detailed information he had about my family. It was all there, in

Aunt Melanie's letter; she had given him the story of my life. And there I had been, puzzled and amazed at how much the British knew.

Finally, a steam locomotive whistled in the distance and bells were ringing, announcing my train and telling the people to step back from the edge of the platform. There were no crowds, no pushing to get on the train, as had been the case during the war. It seemed things were back to normal, at least on this happy day. Still, I didn't waste any time climbing aboard and plunking myself down at a window; I wanted to see the countryside, this time through the eyes of a free man. It was a relaxing ride. I sat back and enjoyed watching the farms and little villages pass through my field of vision as the train chugged along. Yet, despite this new feeling of happiness and contemplation, I couldn't help envisioning a fighter plane coming in low over the horizon, blasting away at our locomotive with machine guns. These were fixations of the mind, I knew; it would take time to forget them.

The Frankfurt station was enormous, bustling with people—civilians and military—rushing back and forth, coming and going. Walking through the large inner hall, I looked for the spot where I had been standing with my British escort less than a week before, waiting for the American MPs to take us to Oberursel. I saw the place and couldn't help think how fast situations can change, and how unpredictable fate could really be. I hopped the trolley for the stop nearest Saalburgstrasse and the address I was looking for. My aunt Edith had alerted the German family I would be checking in with that I was coming, so my arrival was no surprise to them. I received a friendly welcome. Though food was still in critically short supply, my hosts provided me with my first home-cooked meal in ages. Since the lady of the house was employed as a servant by an American family, she received occasional gifts of foodstuffs from her employer, and that made a big difference in what she was able to put on the family dinner table, which happily included me this night.

I also got to satisfy my longing for a real bath, to sit in a full tub of hot water and soak until the water got cold. My neck was awfully dirty from the new uniform I picked up before my discharge. It was an American uniform that had been dyed black, the kind normally issued to prisoners, except the letters "PW" had not been stenciled on the pant legs and the backs of the shirt and jacket. I liked it despite the color; the cut and fit was sharp, sporty, and American. I looked like a real G.I. The black dye was now haunting me, however. It wasn't very permanent and came off to the touch, dirtying my hands, wrists, neck, face, and every bit of skin it came in contact with. I put my British uniform on again after taking my bath. I liked that outfit, too, except I had finally wound up with a pair of those trousers that had a large yellow patch sewn on the front of one leg, covering the hole the British had cut into the cloth. Agreeing with me that "those pants have to go," the landlord's wife boiled my black outfit before I lay down to rest for the night.

Sleeping in their empty featherbed made me feel I was in heaven. Everything around me was so soft and clean smelling; it didn't take me long to fall off into a deep sleep. I slept soundly that night, no nightmares, no dreams, no thoughts of anyone or anything, just one solid period of complete relaxation; just what I needed. When I opened my eyes in the morning, the sun was shining and my black uniform was hanging there neatly pressed. I couldn't believe all this was for real. My host family had gone to work before I woke up, leaving a note with instructions for me to help myself to some bread and jam before going to the I.G. Farben Compound to look up my aunt.

Before leaving my host's apartment, I spoke with Edith's husband Werner over the phone, and he gave me directions how to get to the visitor's gate of the American compound. This was a fenced-in area that housed the headquarters of United States Forces, European Theater, as well as the billets and homes for the large staff of Allied military personnel and civilians, including their families. Werner agreed to fetch me at the gate and take me to his office on Falkensteiner Strasse, where I would meet Edith and their daughter Karin. I was looking forward to seeing all of them again. The last time I had been in their company was two years before, during the latter part of 1944 when I was home on furlough. Much had transpired during these two years. I knew they would have a lot to say. I hopped a streetcar, getting off near the visitor's gate not too far from the Eschenheimer Tower.

The gatehouse was located in a mini-park on the southern side of the high fence surrounding the compound. When I walked in from the street, I saw uncle Werner standing inside, waiting. He had entered the pass office from the opposite side. We were smiling and laughing, I with tears in my eyes, as we gave each other hearty handshakes. Registering for a daytime visitor's pass was simple; the American security people manning this station accepted my POW Discharge as valid identification after I explained I had just been released and had two more days to register with the Police. We walked through the military enclave for several blocks until we reached Falkensteiner Strasse, where Edith was in charge of one of several billeting offices that had been established within the compound. Her office was responsible for housing assigned to U.S. and Allied military personnel and their families.

Tears flowed freely as Edith and I embraced. Cousin Karin didn't quite know what to make of her mother's strange behavior; she had forgotten me, for she had been too young to remember my last visit home. After regaining our composure we all settled down over a strong cup of real American coffee to update each other on our lives. I was happy that Werner had been able to get out of Berlin and make it to the American lines and to our home, and that his whole family had been permitted to accompany the American troops westward during their evacuation of central Germany at the end of June 1945. But I was gravely concerned over the fate of my mother and sister; they had stayed behind and were now stuck in the Russian Zone. There was no legitimate way for them to get out now.

We all agreed that my first order of business would be to register with the police; this was a prerequisite to receiving ration coupons for food, which was in extremely short supply. Edith and Werner offered to see if the engineering section of the Frankfurt Military Post would hire me as a furnace attendant to service the houses in their assigned district of the compound.

The Resident Registration Office at the Police Station would not effect my registration in the absence of a *Zuzugsgenehmigung*, a permit to move to Frankfurt which only the local housing office could issue. We knew it would be impossible to get the permit without presenting evidence of employment, so the job hunt had to take precedence over anything else. Luckily, the Army engineers agreed that a furnace attendant would be a necessity now that cold weather was approaching, and they agreed to hire me. The USFET Personnel Office prepared a letter for me to give to the German authorities, stating I would be hired upon receipt of authority to live in Frankfurt. In the meantime we had located a place for me to live, not far from the compound.

When everything was firmly nailed down, I applied at the Frankfurt Housing Office for the coveted *Zuzugsgenehmigung*. No luck. The bureaucrat required evidence of current employment, not a mere promise of future employment. No matter how hard I tried, I made absolutely no headway with this high-strung and duty-bound German official. Totally frustrated and fuming with anger, I gave him a dirty look, wheeled about, and departed. The next day I reported back to the civilian personnel officer, who did not appreciate the Germans' lack of cooperation and promptly phoned the Office of Military Government for assistance. When he hung up, he instructed me to report to the Frankfurt Liaison and Security Office to pick up and deliver a letter to the local housing office. The Army officer who handed me the sealed envelope suggested I advise Dr. Koenig, the German official in charge, that I would be waiting for his reply.

The letter, which I delivered a day later, consisted of a single sentence. It read: "You are directed to issue authority to live in Frankfurt/Main *(Zuzugsgenehmigung)* to Mr. Walter Schroder."

I waited in the hallway for less than fifteen minutes before the door to one of the offices opened and I was handed my written permit to reside in Frankfurt. Though I was highly satisfied and impressed with the results, the incident was for me a live demonstration of the power and authority of the military authorities now controlling Germany.

My registration with the police followed in short order. The information divulged on the questionnaire I had to fill out would be used in the "Denazification" process; there was a systematic check done of each registered resident's party affiliations and political activities. Penalties were prescribed for willfully withholding or omitting essential information. The intended result was to purify or "denazify" Germany, to make normal people out of Nazis.

The process was more far-reaching than the investigation and identification of criminals and ranking Nazis, however. It went hand in hand with total demilitarization prescribed for the country, prohibiting marching, parades, the wearing of uniforms, singing of military songs and national anthems, glorification of war in books and films, and also forbade the formation of veterans' organizations as well as the production of militaristic toys.

Because of the many atrocities committed by irresponsible German elements, the Allies were operating under a theory of collective guilt, making all Germans—men, women and children alike—personally responsible for these excesses. Whether or not we agreed with their generalized blame-placing was of no consequence; the dictates of the victors prevailed, regardless. With this collective guilt policy in place and understood, however, the combined demilitarization and denazification processes became more understandable, even to those who couldn't accept the arbitrary position of the occupiers.

Getting squared away administratively with local authorities kept me busy, but there were other things of equal or even greater importance that had to be addressed simultaneously. Within days of my arrival in Frankfurt I checked in with the American Consulate in an effort to clarify my citizenship status. The consular officials took a special interest in my case, and I quickly became a regular visitor to their offices at 11 Bockenheimer Anlage. Even though any official position in this matter could only be taken by the State Department in Washington, the local representatives were convinced I had a valid claim to United States citizenship, saying I could be officially American as early as 12 September. Armed with this information, I had registered with the police listing myself as an American citizen. On the ID card issued subsequently by the Frankfurt city authorities, I was represented as such, subject to presentation of a valid U.S. passport, for which application was already pending with the State Department.

In the meantime, I had been hired as a fireman, responsible for attending the furnaces in a string of buildings under administration of the billeting office operated by my aunt Edith and her husband Werner. Every morning around seven o'clock, a contingent of American troops marched through the nearby plaza, sound-

Allied convoys were rolling through towns and hamlets; there was hardly a place where war had not left its mark. (*Imperial War Museum, London*)

Camp 2228 with tents as far as the eye can see. The ten-meter-wide forbidden neutral zone in front of the barbed wire fence soon became known as "the death zone." (*Gilbert Debecker, Belgium*)

"Pussy," Gerberding, and I ham it up during a break in GI training in Marburg, spring 1948. (*Author's collection*)

My first assignment as a GI: the EUCOM Engineer School in Murnau, 1949. (*Author's collection*)

Reunited in West Germany with Mother and Sister. (*Author's collection*)

Father, officially declared a war casualty in 1981, more than thirty-five years after the war. (*Author's collection*)

Coming "home" on the ship *General Hodges* after service in the armies of the Third Reich and the United States, December 1951. (*Author's collection*)

Culmination of a career: Rear Admiral Benjamin F. Montoya, Commander, Naval Facilities Engineering Command, awards the Navy's Superior Civilian Service Medal to Walter Schroder during a May 1989 ceremony at the Naval Construction Battalion Center, Davisville, Rhode Island. (*U.S. Navy*)

ing off to the cadence of one of their NCOs. Sometimes they would even be preceded by a marching band. It was exciting to see and hear the passing column, and I made it a point to be working in that vicinity early in the morning, to be sure I wouldn't miss the procession.

When I was first hired, I had picked up a one-day visitors pass to the compound each morning on my way to work. Now, with the overall registration process completed, I was finally able to apply for a permanent gate pass for civilians. This identification also included a space for insertion of the bearer's nationality. Again, I listed "American." Now there was no longer a need to enter and exit the compound via the visitor's gate for the daily registration process, so I used the gate at Adickes Allee and Eckenheimer Landstrasse; it was closer to my new Oederweg address.

The gates were manned by men of the 508th Parachute Infantry, the unit originally chosen as honor guard for the headquarters of General Eisenhower, Supreme Commander, Allied Expeditionary Forces, which maintained its offices in the I.G. Farben Building. These men were the sharpest soldiers I had ever seen. Their dress and bearing was immaculate; their trousers and Ike-jackets were pressed with creases like knife blades, and they wore white parachute scarves and crisp white gloves. Their spit-polished trooper boots sparkled, accented by white shoelaces. These paratroopers were impressive. With a total of 192 general officers living in the immediate vicinity, one could understand the need for such an elite unit.

During a pass check, one of the guards questioned why I, an American, was carrying a gate pass for indigenous personnel, when I should have been issued an AGO card. I didn't even know what an AGO card was. The guard pulled his wallet and showed me his GI ID Card; it had been issued by the Adjutant General's Office, referred to as AGO. "Oh, that's only for you fellows who just came over from America," I told him. "The card I carry is for those of us who live on the German economy."

"Who in his right mind would want to do that?" he asked me incredulously. I looked at him, smiled, shrugged my shoulders and walked away. He certainly had a point.

As a matter of routine, bags and bundles carried by civilian workers were checked as they left the compound on their way home each day. The critical food shortage among the civilian population outside the compound left little doubt in anyone's mind that those working for the Americans were prone to engaging in black market activities or even stealing from their employers. Taking even a bona-fide gift from the premises was an impossibility. The only way an indigenous employee could carry anything out of the gate would be for the American employer or donor to transport the gift through and beyond the checkpoint.

I spent much of my spare time at my aunt's place inside the compound, where her family had been assigned a furnished single-family house. We usually met there for lunch, and again after work, for supper. Often, especially when our food supply was low, Werner and I would take advantage of the meal offered the workers at the civilian mess hall a few blocks away. The fare was much the same each day: hash or chipped beef, mashed potatoes made from dehydrated spuds, a canned vegetable, and, for dessert, instant pudding and a cup of coffee. Everything tasted so artificial, but who were we to complain or judge? The occupation forces were filling our bellies. We were more fortunate than many, for our relatives in America sent us packages of food. We always forwarded some to my mother and sister in the Russian Zone, since their plight was many times worse than we could even hope to imagine.

One day, after receiving a package from America containing, among other things, a can of dehydrated eggs, Werner proposed cooking up a batch of eggs at home instead of going to the mess hall. That sounded super and we sat down at the table in anticipation. Opening the can, he let out a sly laugh. "I can't believe this—the can is stuffed with cigarettes!" We all jumped up to see for ourselves. What a surprise; cigarettes for Werner and nothing for us to eat. We all joined in the laughter, though. With the cigarettes, Werner could barter for tomorrow's food if need be.

Having registered and applied at the Consulate for a passport entitled me to receive a monthly food subsidy as a "Displaced Person." Being categorized as such felt awkward, since I couldn't identify my situation with the thousands—perhaps millions—of foreigners who had been brought to Germany during the war as volunteer and forced laborers, and were now waiting in refugee camps to be repatriated to their home countries. Somehow, I didn't feel the D.P. designation pertained to me. Still, I could not force myself to decline the periodic supply of cheese, butter and other food staples, so necessary to our well-being.

During a visit to the Consulate on 14 October, Vice Consul McAvoy registered me under the provisions of the Selective Service Act. After I had taken the oath, another consular official questioned the propriety of the Vice Consul's action in the absence of the required clearance from Washington. The registering officer made it clear there was absolutely no doubt in his mind that I was subject to the United States military draft provisions, and that his action was therefore appropriate and proper. After this, I felt I had been reborn an American, though somewhat prematurely. Soon after, *Stars and Stripes,* the daily newspaper for the armed forces, reported that U.S.-born Germans eighteen 18 years of age residing in Germany could enlist in the U.S. army, providing they could prove their American citizenship and pass a thorough investigation to establish their political and moral fitness for service. I picked up on this news item quickly and reported to the Consulate that I might wish to consider the military enlistment option as soon as the citizenship issue was settled.

During the early months of 1947, the Frankfurt Police insisted I request a foreigner's pass if I had intentions of staying in Germany for any length of time while living off the economy. To support the application, I was expected to present an American passport, which I couldn't do since my case was still under consideration in Washington. I explained this on my application, and in reply I was requested by the Police to appear in person to review the matter. The discussion did not take very long. "Do you have an American Passport?"

"Not yet."

"When do you expect to get it?"

"Perhaps in a few more months."

"We cannot issue a foreigner's pass to you without seeing the passport, and without it, you have no proof that you are an American. We therefore have no alternative but to change your ID Card to reflect that you are a German national." With that statement, he stamped "Deutschland" in bold letters over the nationality block of my ID card. Now I was a "confirmed" German. Although the action of the police official annoyed me and I was boiling from within, I remained outwardly calm, feeling deep down that better days would be coming.

Aunt Edith gave birth on 7 March 1947 to a baby boy she named Peter. While she was immobilized at her home, Werner and I took turns taking care of her and the baby the best we could. I stayed overnight at their place inside the military compound on occasion, even though it was not allowed. I reasoned there was no real infraction, since I worked for the occupation forces during the day. As a U.S. citizen waiting for clearance to return to America, I felt confident I wouldn't get into trouble.

The Public Prosecutor's Office for the State of Hesse ruled during the summer of 1947 that I was not affected by the existing denazification and demilitarization laws. This was one more positive step in the right direction for me. Meanwhile, at the Nuremberg war crimes trials, crushing verdicts were being handed down, resulting in hangings and long term imprisonments for certain members of Germany's Nazi hierarchy. To me, these actions represented the final settlement, the squaring of accounts by the Allied powers with the leading functionaries of the now defunct Hitler regime. World War II, merciless and ugly as it had been, was finally over.

During the latter part of November I reported to the Consulate, where I was advised that my passport application had been approved and I now would have to decide whether I wanted to go to America, or apply for enlistment in the U.S. Army of Occupation, taking basic training right in Germany. As much as I had been longing for the chance to return to America, I also felt very comfortable and at home in Germany. I had grown up here and knew the place and the people. Besides, my family was in the Russian Zone, and something had to be done to get them out. Just what I could do from America, I didn't know, but from within Germany, there might be opportunities. My assigned Vice Consul agreed that enlistment in the U.S. Army would be the right thing to do under my particular circumstances. He told me my passport would be issued and held at the Consulate pending my enlistment. Unable to pay the processing fees for the passport in American dollars, I signed my very first promissory note that day, obligating myself to repay the Department of State for the $9.00 they advanced.

For years now, I had been totally immersed in interrogations, interviews, and investigations into my background and activities, as well as those of my family. This, combined with the prevailing political climate of the times, prompted me from the very beginning of my POW experience to retrace and document the time of my youth. It was not surprising, then, that I was able to respond accurately and quickly to the questions posed by members of the Counter Intelligence Corps prior to my enlistment in the U.S. Army. I supported my verbal statements with certified documents from schools, as well as municipal and police authorities from places where I had been registered and known. The American agents, though stern and unsmiling, were nevertheless impressed; I could tell from their facial expressions as I handed them the documents, one by one. They knew as well as I that all they had to do was verify the authenticity of the documentation I presented to them.

A few weeks later I was summoned to Headquarters, European Command, at the I.G. Farben Building, and handed a set of orders with instructions to report to the 7720 EUCOM Replacement Depot for enlistment in the U.S. Army.

8

A New Beginning

The idea of enlisting in the American Army was thrilling; this was a time of anticipation and of happiness. Good fortune had been on my side all along, and now I was being afforded a new beginning, a chance to break with the past and start all over. How lucky I was, in spite of my earlier concerns and doubts about tomorrow and the future.

Once again I was at the *Bahnhof* in Frankfurt, this time waiting for the train that would take me back to Marburg where I had been discharged as a prisoner of war. Now, just seventeen months later, I was returning under a completely new set of circumstances; I would be joining the ranks of my former captors. My life was so confusing, it made my head spin. I hoped things would stabilize soon, so I could once again see clearly and know where I belonged.

As instructed, I called the military base on my arrival at the Marburg station. A short time later an Army truck pulled up. The German civilian driver told me he would be taking me to the Replacement Depot. We chatted along the way. I asked about the place I would be reporting to, while he tried to satisfy his curiosity about how his seemingly unremarkable German passenger could be enlisting in the U.S. Army. He couldn't figure it out, and it took a condensed recitation of my life story to make him understand the circumstances.

He dropped me off at the mess hall. I barely stuck my head

through the door, when a few GIs standing in back of the serving counter called, "Right over here, buddy. Come and get it." Once again that feeling of awkwardness came over me as I walked toward the counter.

The mess sergeant gave me a friendly greeting. "Hi, we've been waiting for you. How about a nice piece of steak? Just put your suitcase down, and come on up to the counter. You must be hungry."

I was starving, ready to eat a horse. "Yes, I am ready to eat," I replied. My eyes almost popped out of their sockets when they handed me a large partitioned tray with two steaks and fried onions on it, along with mashed potatoes, peas, and carrots. Then there was apple pie with cheese, bread, and all the butter I wanted to take, and also a big mug of coffee. I thanked the fellows in white aprons and hats behind the counter. They responded with a friendly smile, as I walked to my table with my first serving of real Army chow. The two steaks were unreal; I couldn't believe my eyes. And were they tasty! I ate quickly at first, gobbling my food down nervously. But after a while I was beginning to have a hard time putting it all away.

The mess sergeant noticed I was slowing down and came over, saying, "I see you're enjoying the steaks."

"You can say that again, sergeant; they're the best I've ever had," I replied.

"When you've had enough, just dump the rest in the garbage bin," he said.

"Oh, no, I can't do that," I replied, aghast. "Food is one thing I've learned not to throw away. I'll finish it; it just might take a little longer."

"Be my guest, don't rush it," he said. "There's more pie and coffee, too, if you want it," and he walked away.

When I carried my empty tray to the scullery, one of the GIs on KP duty remarked jokingly how clean the tray was, and that he'd forego washing it if the corporal weren't watching. I got a kick out of that, and we both laughed.

I spent the first night at the Replacement Depot in a building set aside for transients waiting to be processed. For once, I didn't attract attention; most of the fellows were newly arrived GIs attending their own affairs. Hardly anyone was wearing a proper uniform; most of the fellows wore pieces from different outfits, and nothing matched. No one was paying any attention to the dreary German greys I was hanging around in, either.

There was no roll call for the men in my building the next morning. We just went to the mess hall for early morning chow whenever we were ready. When I got there, I sized up the place, watching the others pick up their trays and utensils and then go through the chow line. That seemed easy, so I followed a bunch of them, imitating every move they made, and soon I was stuffing myself again.

Most of my day was devoted to being processed. Aside from a lot of paperwork, there was a thorough and lengthy physical examination. Later, I was advised there were grooming articles available through the Red Cross office on base. That was an offer I couldn't pass up, for I had no American money to pay for such things, and wouldn't have, until my first payday came around. Finally, I was directed to the supply room to pick up my uniforms and other prescribed GI gear, including an M-1 rifle. Right from the outset I felt I could speak with the supply people; it wasn't like in the Luftwaffe where they just threw things at me. All went well, and by the time I left the supply room, everything fit perfectly. I was delighted; my morale was already very high on this first day in the U.S. Army. I checked in with the Charge of Quarters at my assigned barracks, where I was told to drop my belongings in one of the rooms and then change into fatigues. When I was done, the CQ pointed me in the direction of the drill field with instructions to report to the officer in charge of a group of recruits who were training in that vicinity.

I felt clumsy carrying the M-1 rifle and slung it over my shoulder, not knowing how it was supposed to be carried. All I hoped for was not to meet an officer on the street; I didn't know how to salute with a rifle hanging from my right shoulder; for that matter I didn't know how Americans saluted, period. I made it to the drill field alright, without meeting anyone en route. I saw a small group of uniformed men marching around in the area. As far as I could make out, there was only one officer, a lieutenant, two sergeants and ten or eleven young men, like myself. That was all.

When I reached the group I walked up to the officer smartly and addressed him while standing at attention, "Sir, I am looking for the Recruit Detachment."

"You found it. What's your name?"

"Schroder, Sir; I just arrived."

"OK, lean your rifle against the ones stacked along the side of the field, and fall in with the others."

As soon as I had put up my rifle I joined the squad of recruits who were learning the basics of close order drill. They had arrived a week or two ahead of me, so they were well into their training cycle. One of the sergeants was giving orders: "Left face," "Right face." I quickly joined in, doing it the way I had learned in the Youth movement and the Luftwaffe; it was all the same. The only difference was I couldn't click my heels as I used to. Now I was wearing boots with rubber soles and heels. Gone were the leather soles, hobnails and metal cleats around the heels of the boots I had worn as a Luftwaffenhelfer. But, click or no click, I felt good about my immediate progress and integration.

Next came "About face." As I had learned before, I did an extended left face, turning my body 180 degrees. That's where we differed. All the others turned to the right, kicking their right leg outward, providing the momentum for their 180 degree turn-about. Of course, I bumped into the man next to me who was turning right while I was turning left. Everyone—even the lieutenant, and especially the NCO drill instructors—had a good laugh, asking me to demonstrate the German way several times more. They didn't go for it, but I still thought the way I had learned it originally was the better and easier of the two ways I now knew. No one cared, and I did it the American way from then on.

I was taken off to the side and given a private lesson on the manual of arms, just enough so I knew how to carry my rifle when we marched to the barracks at day's end. After returning to the billeting area, I was able to introduce myself to the others in the squad room where I had left my gear earlier in the day. Our training detachment consisted of a squad of twelve European Enlistees, guys like myself with an American connection who had spent the war years in Europe for one reason or another. There was Gerberding from Germany, who had a very heavy German accent. Then, a fellow from Berlin whose mother was an American. We called him Pussy because of scars on his face that were the result of burns he had suffered during a wartime bombing raid. Then there was Danny from Denmark, and Scotty from Scotland; the remainder, fellows like Hogan, came from England, Ireland and Alsace. Looking around, I had to agree with an instructor's remarks that we resembled a rogues' gallery, America's own Foreign Legion. We took no offense at being referred to as a new breed of mercenaries; we were proud of it and would prove ourselves, given the opportunity. We all had a lot to be thankful for, and we knew it.

Our training was tough. We were kept on our toes, always moving about at quick or double-time and drilling very smartly. There was a general impression at the station that we were officer's candidates. At chow time, we double-timed past the waiting transients, right to the front of the line so we'd be served first. The time allotted on our schedule for eating was shorter than theirs, no more than half an hour, before we headed back for more training.

Nevertheless, we were always laughing and having fun in our group. One day we were lined up with full field packs and the gear needed for a planned hike and overnight bivouac, and one of the assigned sergeants inspected our ranks. In passing in the rear of our line, he checked Gerberding's canteen and found it empty. "Gerberding, what in the hell do you expect to drink in the field— air? Go get some water!" Gerberding's serious, "Vat, mit vater in der canteen?" caused an outburst of laughter. Of course, they couldn't let us get away with it, so we double-timed around the barracks with our field gear on our backs. We still had grins on our faces when it was over, though.

At a later date, Pussy got the lieutenant's goat during a lecture on the operation of our machine guns. After carefully explaining the muzzle velocity of the projectiles and the rate of fire, to impress upon us the deadly capabilities of the machine gun, the lieutenant asked if we had any questions. Pussy was fascinated by the subject; he had been taking notes and making calculations during the entire time the lieutenant was lecturing. He raised his hand, and when cleared to speak, presented a mathematical calculation showing a man could dodge the machine gun's hail of bullets, if he approached the gun at a given speed and at a given angle.

This caught the officer off guard. Not expecting this type of comment, he was flabbergasted and unprepared to dispute the theory offered by one of his recruits. He kept control of the situation, however, by saying, "This would have to be proven in a live setting. Whenever you are ready to make that run, soldier, let me know and I'll get the ammo." Laughter filled the classroom once again. Still, everyone knew Pussy was a crackerjack mathematician, even if he couldn't prove his theory.

Several weeks into our training cycle, when we had learned the basics of American military bearing, we were issued passes to visit the city of Marburg. They were letting us loose; we were real GIs at last. The old university city of 28,500 inhabitants had suffered little war damage. We stuck together as we explored the town, finally ending up at the Red Cross club. None of us had experienced a service club off base, so there was much to observe and take note of before we could feel at ease. There were all kinds of services available, just for the asking. The place was busy. Many GIs spent their leisure hours in the club instead of walking the streets.

As I was making my way through the club, I passed a group of four GIs standing around, chitchatting. One of the fellows looked so familiar, I could have sworn I had seen him before, but where? He must have noticed I had stopped and was staring at him, for he turned my way, looked at me for a moment, then turned away again. But then he turned to look once more. That's when it all came to me; I remembered him, but was not completely sure. I made my way to his side, smiling, my hand extended for a handshake, and asked, "Does 2228 mean anything to you?"

His eyes lit up as he shook my hand, saying, "How in the hell are you? It's been quite a while; nice to see you here."

I replied, "Irving, it's great seeing you, too; this made my day."

His buddies asked if we knew each other. We smiled; all we told them was, "Yeah, we go back a long way," not letting on that we had both been interpreters at POW Camp 2228 in Belgium, two years before. Irving and I talked for a while; he had already been to America, where he enlisted, and now he was back in Germany as a GI. My story wasn't that simple; I hadn't seen the States in over eleven years and now I'd have to wait three more, while serving out my term of enlistment in Germany. He rejoined his buddies when their bus came along to take them back to camp. The goodbyes were short; his "Take care, Walt," and my "See you, buddy," ended our short but memorable chance encounter.

We wrapped up our basic training toward the end of April, when our permanent unit assignments were posted. I was to be transferred to Headquarters 7710 European Command Engineer School in Murnau, Bavaria. No one knew much about Murnau, except that it was south of Munich and north of Garmisch-Partenkirchen. My orders allowed for a layover of three days in Frankfurt. This gave me a chance to drop in on Aunt Edith's family and to look up former co-workers before reporting to my duty station. I celebrated a few fast goodbyes with some of my German friends who were just as excited as I about my becoming an Ami. For the most part, they were getting along pretty well with the Americans, so my new status did not create any animosity. Of course, I detected immediately that my new uniform attracted several young women who previously had paid little attention to me. Now, I no longer had any interest in them.

On my arrival in Murnau I phoned the orderly room and a jeep was immediately dispatched to pick me up. The school was located in the former Kemmel Kaserne, a German artillery post, that occupied some fifty-six acres on the northern end of town. Overall, the school comprised 452 acres, including the Kaserne, a heavy equipment park, a demolition training area and a firing range. When I arrived in front of the headquarters company orderly room, I was met by M. Sgt. Hodge, the first sergeant, who was watering a bed of flowers he had just planted to beautify the barracks area. In a heavy southern drawl he asked if I liked planting flowers. I didn't know if he meant it or if he was joking. "Sure," I said tentatively, "I like planting flowers."

"Then give me a hand out here after you take your duffel bag to your assigned room. The rest of the troops won't be back for several hours anyway."

M. Sgt. Hodge was truly a sharp soldier. He was tall, with

short cropped hair, and he wore a tailored uniform. His shoes were sparkling. He exemplified the soldierly appearance I liked. While we were working together, he gave me a few hints on what he expected of his men in the way of dress and behavior. I listened intently, committing his words to memory.

I was assigned to an empty bunk in a four-man room set aside for school cadre, sharing the space with Corporals Overton and Noel. The fourth bunk also vacant when I arrived, was later assigned to a military student from Turkey. The two GIs in my room were instructors assigned to train students from the American and Allied armed forces—as well as German civilians working for the Americans—in the operation, maintenance, and repair of Army heavy equipment. The school also offered courses on demolitions and mine warfare as well as on a host of related military engineering subjects.

Because of my knowledge of German, I was assigned to the civilian detachment, a cluster of three two-story buildings arranged in horseshoe fashion, which housed transient Germans. Our detail was headed by 2d Lt. Starling, who was subsequently replaced by Lt. Mickey, a P-38 fighter pilot who had battled Messerschmitts over Schweinfurt. Four German civilians, and a former major from Poland who had spent several years in Murnau as a prisoner of war, manned the office and an "indigenous supply room," supervised by a senior U.S. Army sergeant. My job was to interpret for my on-site superiors and to translate written housekeeping instructions from English into German for the benefit of the indigenous student body that was periodically rotated and replaced by crews of newcomers.

The Germans, though civilians, were required to keep their rooms and beds shipshape, GI-style, for the duration of their stay at the school. The student billets were inspected by the NCO, whom I accompanied. Deep down I had to chuckle when telling the Germans, some veterans of the recently concluded war, how to make their beds "the American way," with corners folded precisely and the blankets stretched so tightly that a coin would bounce if dropped on it. Some of the fellows did a perfect job; but others objected to our militaristic approach. That's where I came in, explaining the need for uniformity and discipline in any organizational structure, civilian or military, whenever large numbers of people are involved. Health and sanitary considerations were also stressed in the impromptu lectures I gave in the rooms, the hallways, and at times in the office. I usually brought my former comrades around without much additional fuss, smiling and reminding them how fortunate they were that the Amis were holding back on inspecting their wall lockers.

Shortly after my arrival, a full field inspection was ordered for the cadre. This was the first time some of the old-timers had ever dragged out their field packs and shelter halves and all the other equipment they were responsible for, to look it over and scrub and polish, as needed. How lucky I was, having just completed basic training; this type of inspection had become a weekly routine for me as a recruit, and all of my stuff was spic and span, polished to the hilt. There was nothing for me to do, so I polished the insteps of my leather low-cut shoes, a habit still with me from my days in the German army. That didn't go over too well with my roommates. "What in the hell are you doing, Schroder? Who in the world ever told you to put shoe polish on the insteps of your low-quarters?" I replied that it just made my shoes look neater, and besides, it covered up any dirt that might be in the cracks. I heard a few chuckles, but everyone continued doing his thing the way he had been taught.

Eventually I served as interpreter at court-martial sessions whenever German witnesses were being called. On my first assignment I had a hard time finding out what the protocol was for interpreters. The most I was able to glean was that I should translate everything "exactly" as stated by the witnesses. In the first case at hand, a German who'd driven a truck with two GIs aboard was asked the question "Who was aboard the truck?" He answered as follows: "Cpl. Garry, Pvt. Smith, and I." I translated the driver's response to the court-martial panel of five officers, exactly as stated by the driver.

At that moment, Capt. Morrill, a member of the court, jumped out of his seat, yelling, "What in the hell were you doing there, Schroder?"

I stuttered, "Sir, the 'I' in this instance is the witness, the driver of the truck. Not me." The officers on the panel and even the witnesses laughed so hard they had to call a short recess in the proceedings. I had faced and handled well my "baptism of fire" as an interpreter for the U.S. Army. Any assignment after that was a cinch, including service as interpreter for the area military governor during a daytime raid on a suspected black market center in town, and during negotiations between Lt. Col. Armogida (the school commandant) and the Buergermeister of Murnau over the proposed building of a hotel just outside the Kaserne. Hanging out with our detachment of Special Police and maintaining communication with local police officials was another way my language knowledge came in handy.

I took our stated role as ambassadors of democracy seriously, accepting with pleasure an assignment as the Ami representative to the local GYA, the German Youth Activities organization. My role was to act as liaison between the school and the organization, and to assist the organization in carrying out its youth programs. Army personnel used school resources to build a ballfield and an ice-skating rink for the local children; made busses available to transport the children to various competitions in nearby towns; and donated gifts for the children at Christmastime, including chocolate, candy and toys. In helping this program along, I knew I was furthering the aims of the Allied powers, but also that I was extending a hand to the people with whom I had deep-rooted bonds.

It was mainly on weekends that we were able to let our hair down. A pass, a night club, and a drink with a girl, then a dance and another drink were the ingredients for the fun we were seeking. But woe to any man who broke our unit's perfect VD record; he was sure to be condemned to occupy special quarantine quarters reserved especially for those who wouldn't play it safe, jeopardizing the health and safety of their comrades and of the girls who traded their favors for nylons, perfumes and other scarce commodities. Because everyone knew it was a "no-no" to risk the school's VD-free record by getting the clap, a black market for penicillin shots sprung up in Murnau, frequented by men who suddenly found themselves in trouble. Though the dispensing of shots by German entrepreneurs using reconstituted penicillin was unlawful and frowned upon by our medical staff, some of the GIs chanced a trip to a local civilian source of supply in favor of turning themselves in and having to face the humiliation their peers were sure to dole out. When a sad-faced and nervous soldier approached me from time to time asking me to come to town with him to do the negotiating, I couldn't very well turn down that new-found friend and buddy in distress. I congratulated myself, though, whenever I succeeded in convincing one of them to go on sick call instead, to receive proper treatment.

My evenings and weekends could be pleasureable just hanging around town with a few buddies. We'd spend an hour or two at a *Gasthaus* on the main drag with Pfc. Miller, our postal clerk, playing the piano; or we'd hike to the Staffelsee, just down the hill behind the train station. We always enjoyed the camaraderie. And, when one of our natural strongmen had lifted too many beers and began zigzagging along the sidewalk, I made it a point to get him off the street fast, and back to the barracks. It would keep him out of trouble, and help preserve the image we were so anxiously trying to impress upon the Germans.

Many of us congregated on weekend evenings at the Castle Club, our Army-run, Corps of Engineers enlisted men's club, situated on a little hill just outside the barracks gate. Even though I didn't know a single dance step, I just loved being there, sitting and listening to the band playing Glenn Miller; oh, how fascinating it was to see the guys dance the jitterbug and boogey-woogey. It was crazy, but so *American*—that's why I enjoyed it so much. I hadn't seen anything like it in Germany before. I wished I, too, knew how to toss the girls around like the other guys, but I was still a bit bashful and timid when it came to doing unfamiliar things like that.

There came a time when the samba became popular among our troops. That looked easy and I finally got up enough nerve to grab my date and head for the dance floor. Did I ever kick my heels! What fun it was—until I kicked M. Sgt. Steen (one of our senior sergeants in the school hierarchy) in the shins. I was wearing high-laced trooper boots, my personal trademark of a soldierly appearance, which didn't help. Steen lost his temper. Holding his leg, he ordered me off the dance floor. Good thing the band was blaring away. Embarrassed though I was, not too many of my buddies had seen or heard what had happened. From then on, I stayed off the dance floor whenever Steen showed up.

While in a *Gasthaus* in town during summer festival time, I joined a group of young Germans I'd met before and had a few beers. We were laughing and joking around, they telling me I'd be burning up my rubber soles, running, if the Russians decided to take over, and me getting back at them with some smart remark of my own. While this was going on, an old-timer sitting alone at the table behind me kept mumbling he'd never sit with an American, because they were just no good. He wanted to be sure I got his message, for he kept repeating himself, a little louder each time. Finally, I turned around, got up, and sat down at his table. My young German friends were telling me to let him be, that he was just an old man and didn't mean it. I told them to relax; all I wanted was to talk with the man. I asked the old-timer what he had against the Americans and he replied, "They are just no good, they ought to go home and leave us alone."

"What about the Russians, what do you think of them?"

"They, too, are no good."

"And the British and French, what about them?"

"They are no better."

Now I knew where I stood. I drew a few comparisons between the Russians and the Americans, drawing on things I remembered from the war years. Eventually, he agreed the Americans were the best of the four occupying powers and the Russians the least desirable. That satisfied me, and I bought him a beer. "The Americans aren't that bad after all, don't you think?"

"I guess you're right," he said.

I then rejoined the others, who complimented me on the way I had handled the situation.

About that time, on 26 June 1948, the Soviet occupation forces created some very tense moments for us when they closed all overland supply routes to Berlin, preventing access to the city from the Western Zones of Occupation. This meant the two-million people living in the sections of the city occupied by the Western powers would soon be without essential food supplies, unless the barriers were lifted without delay. They were not lifted, and our forces had to resort to airlifting critical foodstuffs to the Berliners as an interim measure.

Meanwhile, we were getting ready for something bigger. We were engaging in day and night exercises, riflepractice, hiking, and attending demolitions training at our own school, under Capt. Dennis and Sfc. Carey, both whizzes in their field. Many of us were itching for action, even though we knew our position was far from secure, and the Soviets had more big stuff on line and ready for action than we did.

About the same time, our ranks were increased through the addition of a number of recruits from the States, all kids younger than myself. To them, I was an old-timer at twenty. I suppose I did have quite a bit of prior experience which neither they nor even my best friends knew about. Nevertheless, the kids soon heard of my language skills, prompting several to let me know they'd be looking for me to join them when they headed for the mountains, should things go haywire. Early on, we knew we might not make it out of Germany if the Russians steamrolled Europe with their massed tanks. And faced with capture by the Russians, we would have opted to becoming partisans, sniping away at them at every opportunity.

For the duration of my stay in Murnau, I had been sending small one-pound food packages to my mother and sister in the Russian Zone. Nothing larger than a pound was allowed into the area controlled by the Soviets, but there was no objection to sending up to eleven one-pound packages at a time, so I tied them together. It worked; Mother received them, and I had beaten the system. I was ordering coffee and chocolate syrup from the States by the case, and repacking and mailing the cans as soon as they arrived. The increasingly hostile attitude of the Soviets in what we were beginning to refer to as the Cold War, sent chills running down my spine; I was ever more aware of the explosiveness of the situation and of the extremely precarious position my family was now in. Things had been bad enough before, but now the ominous political climate left me with much to think and worry about.

On one of our training days during the latter part of July, the first sergeant told me not to go on a scheduled field exercise with my company, for a member of the Counter Intelligence Corps would be coming and wanted to see me. All I could say was, "Oh, brother, now what?" and I stood by, waiting.

9

Iron Curtain

E arly in the morning, most of our personnel took off in a long truck convoy for a field exercise to test their skills in preparing a bridge for demolition. I stayed behind as instructed, waiting to meet with the man from the CIC. I couldn't figure out what he might want; I knew he would be involved in security matters, but other than that, I knew very little. Before long, one of the fellows from our orderly room came looking for me to tell me I had a visitor waiting. I headed for the orderly room. There was a man standing in the hall, wearing civilian clothes; he was smiling. "Walt Schroder? I'm Agent Jack, how are you today?"

"I'm fine, Sir, how are you?"

"You don't have to 'sir' me, just call me Jack, and I'll call you Walt, OK?"

That was fine with me; anything was fine with me as long as I wasn't in some kind of trouble.

Jack suggested we hop in his car and ride over to our headquarters building near the main gate to find a place where we might sit and talk in private. While driving, he told me he had heard I was doing very well and that especially my interpreting work had prompted words of praise from several of the officers at the school. I hadn't been aware of the attention that was being paid to my performance. His report was encouraging. After settling down in one of the empty classrooms, Jack asked if I could assist him by making occasional translations of documents and letters of a diversified nature, so he could get a better idea of their contents. I agreed.

He continued by inquiring how I was getting along personally during these times of tension and uncertainty, with my mother and sister "over there in the Russian Zone." I let him know exactly what I knew and how I felt. I volunteered that I had set up a maildrop at the local address of a reliable *Sudeten* German through whom all mail between my mother and myself was being routed. Short of opening and censoring the mail, no one on the other side would know my mother had a son who was a GI in West Germany. With the Soviets there, and the new wave of greed and hatred among the people, I just wouldn't want to jeopardize the safety of my family by having them receive American GI mail. I noticed Jack had a slight smile on his lips as I was telling him of my concerns and what I was doing about them.

With my folks, the food situation had been the most critical problem all along, a real crisis. My mother's three sisters in America were keeping them alive by sending packages, one after the other, containing the vital necessities she, my sister and my grandma so desperately needed. But the shipments were not being allowed to flow freely. First of all, only packages from the other Occupation Zones in Germany were permitted to enter the Russian Zone, none directly from America, and those let in were limited to one-pound each. To get around this restriction, our relatives in the States were sending larger packages to Aunt Edith in Frankfurt, who was repacking them into the smaller one-pound parcels and sending them onward. The process was tedious, unfair, and a willful obstruction, ridiculous at a time when people were starving. Nevertheless, as long as there was a steady flow of packages, the word my relatives and I had gotten was that my folks in the Russian Zone were doing OK. However, any disruption—such as a longshoremen's strike—was enough to create a new panic situation, causing frantic calls for help.

Jack listened intently, and I took the opportunity to also let him know some of my deeper concerns. Mother's letters to me and to her sisters, begging for help and expressing feelings of having been forsaken, were eating away at me. "I could have cried," she wrote, "I was so discouraged. No wood, no coal, the bread all gone. . . . We have become so uncultured and tactless, more like animals than human beings, in our search for the things that sustain our lives. We don't want to die of hunger, but we have lost respect even for the things in our surroundings that are good. . . ." I told Jack that I was frustrated; I wanted to do something, but my hands were tied.

In her desperation, Mother had offered to give up her daughter for adoption to her sisters in America, just to get the child out of her present surroundings and circumstances. She had even tried filing immigration applications at one point, but was advised that applications from the Russian Zone could not be accepted as long as the United States did not have consular representation in that area. Yet, despite all the hardships and setbacks they were experiencing, Mother was still maintaining a positive outlook about eventually making it to America . . . somehow. To me, however, it didn't seem they'd ever be let out of the Russian Zone; certainly not while Soviet-American relations were as strained as they presently were.

"Walt, something has to be done to get them out of there," Jack said, "Perhaps there is a way. I know of a young German woman here at the school who will soon be crossing into the Russian Zone to get her three-year-old son out; maybe she can help. She'll have to make it across the border illegally at night, and at great risk and danger, but it's the only way; there are no alternatives." I hesitated a moment, as millions of thoughts were flashing through my mind. Getting them out—yes. But the risks had to be considered very carefully; I could say all I wanted, but it was my mother and little sister who would be taking the chances. They could both be shot at the border by Russian patrols, or wind up in a Soviet concentration camp; I had heard their camps were no different from the places the Nazis had operated, merciless and brutal, without any concern for life. The risks were tremendous.

I was now faced with realities I had personally been able to circumvent; this was one of those situations we consciously put out of our minds and don't think about. But here I was, at a crossroads that would determine the unfolding of our lives from this time forward, and I needed to come up with quick answers. I kept thinking of different scenarios and outcomes. What if they captured my little sister and hauled her off to Russia as an orphan, never to be seen or heard from again? I couldn't bear the thought, and a renewed feeling of helplessness and extreme tension came over me. My jaws were tightening, my muscles felt strained, and my hands were clenched into fists. Finally, I said, "Look, I'll do anything I can from here, but the last word has to come from my mother. It's her life that's at stake; only she can know if the risks are worth the chances she'll have to take. She's the one over there, suffering. I am sure she'll do what is best for her daughter and herself. Let's propose running the border, and see what reaction we get."

For the first time since our meeting, Agent Jack had a serious look on his face. He, too, was concerned. "OK, here it is: get in touch with Fraeulein Krause. She is of medium height, slender, has long brown hair, and is always well dressed. She speaks English fluently, and works in an office near the post theater. See if she can help in arranging something for your family, but be sure you don't scare her off. I'll be in touch in about a week. Let me know then how you made out." We shook hands, once again smiling, and left the room, each going his own way.

First and foremost, I had to locate Frl. Krause and see if she could help; if so, the next step would be to get in touch with mother. Knowing the general area where the young woman worked allowed me to make inquiries about her among the fellows in my barracks who were assigned to the same office. I asked what they knew about the good-looking brunette who worked in their area. One of the guys replied, "You can't make out with that one, Schroder. She sure is built, but she doesn't fool around; she stays to herself."

"Well, I'd like to take a crack at her, anyway. What's her name?"

"Krause, Fraeulein Krause," he confirmed.

Now, I knew for sure where she worked; I could wait for her one day after hours and try to make contact. I didn't put it off too long. The next day I stood across from the Headquarters Building, eyeing the civilian workers passing in front of me as they headed for the gate, and home. Then came Frl. Krause, her appearance exactly as described, a good-looker. Boy, how I'd like to take her out, I thought, but I had more serious business to tend to. Right then, my personal desires were secondary.

Just asking if her name was Krause put a momentary scare into the young woman. And when I told her it was my understanding she would be crossing into the Russian Zone before long, she became fidgety and frightened. She stammered as she spoke. I felt sorry; I wanted to put my arms around her, to hold and reassure her, but instead I said, "Please, don't be afraid. I ask only because I have a problem. I need your help."

At that, she regained some composure. "What do you mean?" she asked.

I knew I was taking a grave chance, telling this girl about my family. I didn't know the woman, nor what her political leanings were. All I knew was that she would be "going over." Maybe she was going there to stay; maybe she was a spy, a courier carrying information to the Russians. How could I know? I had to chance it, to begin having faith in the people around me, so I told her my problem, and asked if she could help.

Her eyes lit up, "Oh yes, I am going to get my son from the other side in another six weeks or so. If you want, I will ask the people who will be taking me across the border to help bring your family out, too. If you give me the address, they will contact your mother from over there and make arrangements."

It was done; I gambled on the young woman's sincerity and gave her the address. We agreed I would contact my mother immediately while she got in touch with her party, and that we would meet again soon to see how things were going.

I got off a letter at once, explaining to my mother in garbled language that she would be contacted from within the Russian Zone shortly regarding her trip. In the meantime, she should be giving serious thought to taking an extended vacation, without spreading the word around. It wasn't too long until I received her reply. She feared the consequences in the event something went wrong. I knew how devastating the outcome could be, but I also knew if she didn't take advantage of this opportunity, there might not be another chance of getting her out from behind the Iron Curtain. My reply reflected my innermost feelings, my calculated judgement based on common sense, and now, also prayer. The next communication from the other side carried a more positive note; they were ready and prepared to run the gauntlet. Without delay, I got word to Frl. Krause, who had also received a favorable reply from her contacts in the meantime. And Agent Jack was delighted at the good news, when I told him.

The burden of breaking up her household on the QT, disposing of the furniture and other belongings in anticipation of fleeing to the West, was one of the many things my mother would have to take care of. Any careless remarks on her part, overheard by an informant, could blow the plan before it ever got off the ground. But, having lived under the scepters of two successive dictatorships that fostered jealousy, treachery and squealing on one's neighbor, she was sensitive to the dangers involved. She knew whom she could trust, and whom not. Quietly, she'd have to approach reliable neighbors, soliciting their interest in her belongings, which would be theirs when she abandoned her apartment. The most critical element in pulling off the plan would be securing train tickets to the border region, into which, I knew, entry was restricted. Only bona fide residents of the towns in the vicinity of the border were allowed to travel into the heavily patrolled areas. With the help of friends, however, the necessary passes and tickets might be secured. It was all a gamble.

Preparations for the trip took weeks and the waiting made me nervous. If they didn't make their move soon, they would have to face the harsh winter weather in addition to coping with the trigger-happy Russian border guards when they did attempt the crossing. Finally, on 20 January 1949, I was handed a telegram. It read: "Arrived Frieda safely; please get us. Signed: Mama." I couldn't believe my eyes. I quickly told M. Sgt. Hinceman, my immediate superior at the civilian detachment, of the news, and asked the first sergeant for emergency leave so I could go to the border to pick up my folks. My request was not unexpected. Within hours I had my leave orders. In the meantime I phoned Uncle Werner in Frankfurt to give him the news, and also Mr. Jasmund, the Army civilian I had worked for before enlisting, to see if he would drive me to the border to pick up my people in his car. Everything clicked perfectly. We met in Frankfurt the next day, and headed out for the town of Frieda, just inside our Zone border near Eschwege.

Although running the border was no longer big news, for many freedom-lovers had done so before, meeting my own mother and ten-year-old sister that day was, to me, the biggest and most important event in our family history. This feeling became clear as we embraced in tears, and again later, when they told of their ordeal getting past the Russians and through the deep tank ditch in the middle of the woods. We got on the road without delay, heading back to Frankfurt with our "visitors." Mother told me she was carrying a copy of my National Service life insurance and my GI photograph with her, just in case she'd been stopped by an American patrol. "Oh, brother," I said, "What if the Russians had stopped you?"

"Oh, gosh, I didn't think of that," she replied.

We laughed heartily along the way; our joy was without measure. At a snack bar along our route, my sister had her first milkshake, ever. It tasted so good to her, but the drinking straw was the fun part. She watched other American dependent children blowing into their straws, making the paper sleeves zoom through the air, laughing. She caught on quickly, imitating the things they did. She too could have fun. A banana split was her next "first," the banana being the strange never-before-seen item in the dish. I felt so sorry for all the deprivation she had suffered, but I knew better times were upon all of us.

Mr. Jasmund allowed us to use one of the Army's vacant apartments in the Frankfurt compound, where we could clean up and spend the night. The next morning, after visiting with Aunt Edith and her family, my folks and I hopped a train for Murnau. On arrival, we walked to the home of one of my German friends, a member of the *Landpolizei*, who had agreed to take them in temporarily.

The three of us went to the *Gemeindeamt* the next morning to register my mother and sister, so they could receive local ration coupons. Once again, I found myself in the middle of a bureaucratic morass. Illegal border-crossers without written permission to be in the state of Bavaria, were not eligible to receive ration coupons. Likewise, they could not be registered with the police, which was a prerequisite to being permitted to live in town. "Where can they get the permit?" I asked.

"They will have to go to Camp Moschendorf, the receiving camp for illegal border crossers, near Hof." That was ridiculous. Under no circumstances would I risk taking them to a camp just fifty kilometers from where they had started out, nor would I risk having some bureaucrat ship them back into the Russian Zone. After being told I could make a personal appeal at the office of the *Landrat,* the district magistrate, I wasted no time reporting to that office, in Weilheim, the next day.

At least this official was open-minded and willing to listen. The meeting concluded on assurance that the written permission for my mother and sister would be issued at Moschendorf, in their absence, and that they could remain in Bavaria until their departure to America, but that the State would not assume any responsibility for their financial or economic support. I accepted the district magistrate's proposal, as the best deal attainable, and took the next train back to Murnau.

Pending settlement of the paperwork issues, Agent Jack offered to put up my two border-runners with his own family of four, in their Army-requisitioned home just north of Garmisch-Partenkirchen. I was overwhelmed at his offer, especially now that my Pfc. pay would have to cover the financial support for Mother and Sister as well. I recognized, however, that having my mother move in with Jack would allow him to pry into her background and pick her brain for eye-witness information on life in the Russian Zone. But, so what, I thought; the humane aspects of Jack's offer far outweighed the less attractive features. Returning his favors in a small way would certainly be a fair enough price to pay for his generosity and what appeared to be a sincere interest and concern for our well-being. Knowing my mother as I did, I was certain she would offer to help around the house, doing those unavoidable daily chores. She wouldn't accept room and board without reciprocating.

Living with a real American family and participating in their daily routine as accepted equals would give my folks an insight into the life that awaited them in the States. Visiting with them at Jack's home on weekends was a rewarding experience for me as well. Jack and his family were generous hosts and true friends, caring about my family without regard to their have-not status. I was delighted when told they had been to Garmisch, shopping, or sight-seeing in the beautiful mountain region. And, when my loved ones showed off the clothes Jack's wife had come up with, I felt the burden on my shoulders becoming lighter.

Luckily, I was offered part-time work, after hours, managing the post theater at the service club. I accepted without hesitation; the pay made up the shortfall in the financial resources I needed to feed and maintain my dependents adequately.

It took until mid-March to secure the needed permits and accomplish the required registration, before I could seriously think of bringing my folks back to Murnau.

We spent a pleasant, quiet and peaceful summer there. It was fun being near each other. But there were serious matters that had to be taken care of, things of consequence to our future and our long-term plans. Sister Annerose attended school, Mother was busy filing her immigration papers, and I carried on with my soldierly duties at the Kaserne.

My peaceful days came to an end when the officer in charge of the civilian detachment insisted I had misled him by saying the GI blankets in the civilian supply room and in the possession of the German students were OK. On the strength of my statement, he had signed the inventory for over 400 blankets, certifying they were in perfect condition. During a spot-check of the German student barracks, however, he noted that there was hardly a blanket without a flaw. Most of the ones he saw had holes in them. The lieutenant was furious and blamed me for having an inventory of defective blankets. He threatened court-martial action if I did not correct or replace the bad blankets, posthaste. I tried to explain that our blankets were categorized Class X, defective, and that these were the only blankets we were able to obtain for use by the civilian students. Furthermore, the blankets were originally accepted as Class X and signed for as such, by his predecessor. My German supply room assistant verified my statements, yet the detachment officer insisted I was at fault for having told him the blankets were OK when they were not. I tried to clarify the matter for him, but to no avail.

Shook up, I mentioned my plight to my mother the next time I saw her. "Is it anything I can fix?" she asked.

"There is at least one small hole, you know, from cigarette burns, in each one of them. Some have more than one, and then there are a few with holes that are a little larger, two centimeters in diameter maybe."

"Why don't you bring a few and let me take a look at them?" she suggested. I latched on to her idea quickly. I grabbed two of the defective blankets the next night after work and headed back into town. She looked at the blankets, saying, "That's nothing; it would be like mending your woolen socks, remember? Bring me a bunch of those, I'll fix them, then go to your lieutenant and see what he has to say. I'm not going to let my big boy get into trouble, not while I'm here!" That mother of mine sure knew how to make me feel better in a hurry, I thought; she always had.

The next day I asked the lieutenant for permission to take a bundle of blankets off base, where my mother wanted to see what she could do to fix them. Surprisingly, he agreed. I got hold of our civilian driver, and after loading a roll of twenty-five blankets onto the detachment's three-quarter-ton truck, we took them into town and dropped them off. Mother did a fantastic job on that batch of old surplus GI blankets, weaving the threads artistically, closing the holes one by one. Of course, the woven places showed up when you spread out the blankets, but there were no more holes. The lieutenant was impressed. He accepted the lot and authorized me to have the rest of them done. After that, I started hauling fifty blankets back and forth at a time, until none of the blankets in the inventory had any holes in them. When all was said and done, I still didn't believe I had done anything wrong. The lieutenant had not taken the time to check the records before he put his signature on newly prepared inventory forms, making him responsible for everything that was listed on them. But no matter who was at fault, I was lucky to have my mother so close by; without her I wouldn't have known what to do.

I saw Jack during that summer whenever he made his routine stops at the Kaserne. One time, he mentioned casually that Munich Military Post Headquarters was in need of an interpreter with German fluency and a good foundation in German military terminology. The assignment, he said, would be with the post S-2, the intelligence shop, and would involve written translations and occasional interpreting, which he felt I could do, hands down. Soon after, a visit to Munich was arranged, where I met Lt. Col. Ryan, the S-2. The job, as he described it, sounded very interesting. There was more to it than the routine translating Jack had spoken of; there'd be opportunities to speak with German POWs returning from Russia, also scientists, and even some disenchanted people who walked in from time to time. The variety of material I would be handling made it sound like the interpreter's position was an important assignment on the staff of the S-2, and challenging, to boot. I told Lt. Col. Ryan I'd be interested in joining his staff as interpreter.

At least two months passed without a single word from anyone, until early in November when I received orders to report for duty to the 7822 Station Complement Unit, McGraw Kaserne, Munich, on Thanksgiving Day.

This meant packing up and going, leaving Mother and Sister behind once again.

10

Now, Go in Peace

Sergeant Vaughn, the mess sergeant for the civilian detachment, drove me to Munich in time to meet my reporting deadline at McGraw Kaserne. After turning in my orders to the Charge of Quarters, I was assigned a room in one of the apartment houses along Tegernseeer Landstrasse, which ran through the post. During the war, the Germans had used several sizeable warehouses within the enclave for a quartermaster facility and storage site; now, the large main building served as U.S. Army Headquarters, Munich Military Post. The troop billets, as well as the officers' and dependents' quarters, were all within a string of three-story houses that lined the main thoroughfare, now closed to the public.

My room was one of three in a small apartment I would be sharing with two other privates first class. One of the fellows, Steve Karadian, was in his room when I arrived, listening to a shortwave radio. During our introduction he mentioned his interests in ham radio operation, and also told me that he worked in the S-2 section, the office to which I was being assigned. Because of our billeting and job relationship we quickly became friends. Pfc. Clark, another of the boys in our office, was billeted in the building next to ours. I met him the next day, after completing the check-in process in Detachment C of the 7822 Station Complement Unit, the outfit to which all of us with duties at post headquarters were assigned for administrative support.

Our offices were located in the city, at Ludwigstrasse 28, one floor above the American Consulate, and next door to the operations section of the 508th MPs. Translating documents and newspaper articles from German to English were among my first assignments. The material was of a diversified nature, covering areas of interest to our forces, including reports on attitudes of the civilian population, activities of left- and right-wing political elements, economic and social data, information on border incidents and displaced persons activities, and also information on the latest rumors circulating among the population. Data of special interest was earmarked for inclusion in the biweekly Intelligence Summary, which the S-2 published at a different site. The wide range of materials assigned to me for translation made the job very interesting and challenging, often even difficult, especially when I was dealing with unfamiliar subject matter.

I focused my greatest attention, however, on interviewing German POWs released by the Russians. While I quizzed them on the work they had performed, the places they had been, and the things they had seen, I was also sure to inquire if they had been captured in East Prussia, the area where my father had been stationed. There had been no word from or about him since my last letter was returned in January 1945, marked "undeliverable." After learning during the Munich interviews of the Soviets' encirclement of large contingents of German troops at Heiligenbeil and Koenigsberg, and the annihilation of the men entrapped in these pockets, I filed a search application with the Bavarian Red Cross, hoping they might be able to shed some light on my father's fate or whereabouts. I later found out they were in touch with the Red Halfmoon of the USSR, the Russian version of the Red Cross, and that all inquiries were being routed to Moscow via the International Red Cross in Geneva, Switzerland. But responses were extremely slow. My distrust of the Soviets from the war years still lingered; not much had changed, really. Now they were at political odds with the Western powers, so I wasn't wrong in having little faith they would respond to a Red Cross query in my behalf. Driven by these deep-rooted inner feelings, I decided to go beyond the service provided by the Red Cross, and I placed an advertisement in the *Suchdienst Zeitung*, a special publication in which the names and particulars of missing and lost Wehrmacht members were listed. I did this in the hope that some returnee would spot and recognize my father's name and get in touch.

Soon after the holidays, Mother received notification she could leave for America—alone. She could not take her daughter, who was a minor. The rules were that she could go, and ask for her daughter following her own arrival in the United States. We were happy and depressed at the same time. What would I do with my eleven-year-old sister once Mother left? I was a GI, on call twenty-four hours a day. How would I take care of her?

The answer came like a miracle, for when Sgt. Vaughn heard of my dilemma, he said, "Schroder, your sister can live with us. We have a big enough house to accommodate one more kid."

"That's fantastic, but what will it take to make it possible?"

"You just pay for the milk she drinks, and forget the rest; leave that to me and my wife Mickey. We'll take care of her while you're in Munich. Just come and see her as often as you can make it." Sgt. Vaughn came through and made good on his promise. He took my sister in.

Ever since I was a child I had enjoyed parades, watching men in uniforms marching in cadence to the beat of a good military band. The precision with which the marchers performed their rifle and close order drills had always been exciting to me, enough so that I wished I could join their ranks. I got my wish on Armed Forces Day, 1950, when our unit participated in a spectacular show of U.S. military might at Theresienwiese, site of the annual Oktoberfest.

Under the motto "teamed for defense," several thousand troops, plus hundreds of tanks, scout cars and trucks, passed in review before a host of senior U.S. military officers and military government officials, while formations of combat aircraft flew overhead. The roaring engines and the clanking of tank-treads combined with the rumbling of a fleet of trucks as they rolled by, were enough to drown out the Army band. Americans and Germans alike lined the parade route to witness first hand the fighting power and muscle of the American Armed Forces in Germany. The men from my unit were among the mounted infantry troops, sitting upright and at attention in their trucks as they followed the tank formations across the Theresienwiese and past the reviewing stand. Looking around, I could tell that each and every man was proud of his role and place.

Just when life was running smoothly, Sgt. Vaughn received orders reassigning him to another station. This meant finding a new place for my sister Annerose to stay. Luckily, Sgt. Denman and his wife, both friends of the Vaughns, were anxious to be of help. The two households were just down the street from one another, which eased the transition for my young sister. By this time my own rotation to America was only six to eight more months away, and little sister should be gone long before that, making the present change of residences a less significant event, a situation that was at least tolerable. As it turned out, the Denmans were fun to be with, or so little sister said.

After a period of administrative swaying and status clarifications at the American Consulate in Munich, she received the green light to immigrate to America, where our mother had been waiting nervously for months. Annerose's departure was scheduled for the first week in August; the news couldn't have come at a better time. On 25 June, South Korea was invaded by outside forces. The U.S. quickly became involved in a police action under the umbrella of the United Nations, but soon found itself embroiled in hostilities of greater magnitude. Once again our training—this time in Munich—was beefed up as we prepared for any eventuality. Seeing my sister off at the Frankfurt airport on 2 August was a blessing and a great relief. It represented the removal of responsibilities I never dreamed I would be able to shoulder, especially not in the environment of military and political uncertainty we constantly found ourselves in.

With Sister on her way, my vow had been fulfilled. I had gotten my loved ones out of the postwar political quagmire of a dictatorship as relentless as that of the Hitler regime, and settled them in America. From here on, they would be at a safe distance from the hot spots of possible confrontation.

As for my own future, I planned on extending my enlistment for one year and reaping the benefits of a fat reenlistment bonus which would pay for a nice long furlough, to Paris maybe, and the Eifel Tower; I'd find a cute mademoiselle and get lost. I was dreaming. Before I could sign on for the additional year and the cash bonus, instructions came through authorizing, by order of the President, the involuntary extension of all enlistments by one year because of what had by then become the Korean crisis. As a result, I had another year to serve, and no reenlistment bonus nor any viable means of getting to Paris. I spent my two-week furlough right in Munich, and had no regrets.

A GI could have a lot of fun in the city; I did. The Army service club at the Buergerbraeu Keller put on a floor show every now and then, and I enjoyed the entertainment tremendously. I really went there, though, to see for myself the scene of a missed assassination attempt. On 8 November 1939, a bomb had gone off near the speaker's rostrum halfway through a speech by the Fuehrer. On the given night, Hitler had for no obvious reason deviated from his usual routine, leaving the hall earlier than anticipated. In so doing, he missed by a mere eight minutes the explosion that could have ended his life and changed the course of history. Now, after the bloody war that might never have been, American GIs were cheering on their entertainers in the very same hall where Hitler had narrowly escaped death eleven years before. And I was in the crowd with them. I couldn't help but ponder the irony of it.

Meeting the right girls—girls who were liberal and fun to be with, yet free of disease—could be problematic. In the center of the city, especially after dark, women abounded. They were of all ages, standing, watching, walking the streets waiting for a GI to proposition them. What we considered "good" or "clean" girls were hard to come by, and the risk of contracting a contagious disease was ever present. Conversely, abstention was considered unmanly, perhaps even un-American, and therefore not really an option. For some of the fellows it was like playing an endless game of roulette, continually risking their health. The losers always got burned.

One of my Detachment C buddies was assigned to the "VD Patrol." His job was to accompany the German Police in rounding up known street walkers and prostitutes, and especially women linked with spreading the dreaded venereal diseases. He knew which girls went into the hospital for observation and treatment, and when they were being discharged "clean." In deference to his buddies he sometimes announced the release dates and times through the grapevine, and then arranged for some of the fellows to befriend the girls before they got back into circulation. I didn't bite and went my own way, using my German to full advantage.

Word got around pretty fast in the Munich detachment that I spoke German fluently. While I was walking in the center of the city one day, a jeep loaded with guys from my unit pulled up alongside me, the driver yelling, "Hey, Schroder, hop in; we need an interpreter." Why not, I thought, and I squeezed into the back seat with the three fellows already there. They were loud and noisy; they were drunk and taking big swigs from an uncorked bottle of whiskey. "Oh, what did I get myself into," I thought.

It didn't take long to find out. The driver miraculously kept the jeep moving along the street in an orderly manner, until, suddenly he jumped the curb, driving the length of the sidewalk. "What the hell are you doing?" I yelled.

"Just tell the Krauts to get out of our way or I'll run 'em down!"

I had no alternative but to start shouting for the Germans to clear our path; I was stuck in the back seat of the jeep, squeezed between the other three. None of us could move, it was so tight back there. I pushed hard and finally managed to free my legs so I could stand up. "Vorsicht!" I shouted, "Machen Sie den Weg frei. Gehen Sie schon weg. Schnell, treten Sie zurueck, bitte. Aufpassen. Achtung, zuruecktreten!" I warned the Germans in various ways to watch their step and to get out of the way.

Oh, how I hated doing this, and we were supposed to be the "ambassadors of democracy," the shining examples of a better order. We muffed that one, but good, I thought to myself. The whole time I was yelling at the Germans to clear the way, I was also blasting our driver with a barrage of tough GI lingo till finally he pulled back onto the street and around the corner and let me off.

"You guys are whacky," I said, shaken up, "really nuts. You ought to get your butts back to the barracks before you get into trouble, and I mean it!" All they said was, "OK, OK," and drove off.

Every now and then our colonel got some static from his civilian operatives, who were being stopped and searched by

German authorities, preventing them from carrying out their assigned duties. These searches compromised the agents and often caused them to lose their effectiveness for later details.

The Colonel called me, saying, "Schroder, I'd like to have some special S-2 IDs designed and printed up for our people, so they won't get stopped and searched. Think you can come up with something?" I agreed, and the Colonel detailed the language he wanted to see on the picture-IDs, which would include a German translation of the provisions.

After the Colonel approved my design for the IDs, I arranged for a German shop to print up a supply of the cards. I picked them up when they were ready. They looked good. I was proud and hurried back to our office on Ludwigstrasse to hand them over to Lt. Col. Ryan. As I made one final check before delivering the cards, I discovered a misprint. I couldn't believe my eyes. This would cost us both time and money, and the Colonel would be peeved. But it was too late to do anything about it. I had to tell him, he was waiting. "Colonel," I began, somewhat meekly, "I made a sad discovery: the cards contain a misspelled word."

"Let me see. Where?"

"In the first sentence, where it says, 'the bearer is empowered to investigate matters and incidents as directed by this office,' the word 'directed' contains a mistake, ending in a 't.' That's a real blooper."

"No, we'll use it to identify any fakes that might show up. I'm sure a counterfeiter would use the correct spelling. That's how we'd know. Tell the desk sergeant to make a record of this."

I was amazed how quickly the Colonel turned a bad situation around to work in his favor. I had learned something.

After working in the main office as a corporal for several months, I was assigned to the S-2 Operations Office, situated in a mansion across the Isar River. We referred to it as "the House." I would live and work there, reporting to the main office only once a day. An elderly German couple occupied the janitor's apartment on the lower level of the building, with the first floor set aside as office space and the second floor as sleeping quarters. Our senior NCO shared the living area with me when he was not off on some assignment. He was there the day I moved in and gave me the grand tour of my new environment. Stopping in the living-room, he said, "See this furniture, the large glass-topped coffee table, the cushion-covered couch and matching wooden armchairs? They all came from Hitler's apartment on Prinzregentenstrasse."

"Come on now, you're kidding me," I said.

"No, it's the Gods-honest truth. The furniture was moved here from Hitler's Munich apartment at No. 16 Prinzregentenstrasse."

I was fascinated and made it a point to try the seats out after I completed the walk-through of my new home.

I was introduced to my co-workers, all civilians, German and Russian. Germans I could understand, but who were the Russians? The Sergeant explained to me in private that one had lived in Russia before the Bolshevik Revolution, one or two had been associated with General Vlasov and the Russian Liberation Army, which had sided with the Germans, and two others had wartime Soviet military experience. All were disgruntled with the Soviet system and the communistic regime that had turned their country into a dictatorship; all had burned their bridges, there was no returning home for any of them. I wasn't able to pick up anything on the two German investigators in the office, except for being told they were trustworthy and completely reliable. In addition, my staff was augmented by two English-speaking secretaries.

The men were normally on the go, picking up local gossip and making contacts with German governmental officials in the area under control of Munich Military Post, which extended to the Czech border in the east, the Austrian border to the south, and embraced the cities of Augsburg, Ingolstadt and Regensburg. In the office, the secretaries translated and typed the reports made by the agents. The proofreading and editing of the final product, the biweekly Intelligence Summaries, was left to me.

It was around this time, in December 1950, that members of the Munich Criminal Police confiscated a suitcase containing Hitler's most personal papers. Some of these had been sought by the Nuremberg war crimes tribunal. The documents had been held in safekeeping by Hitler's former housekeeper, Frau Anni Winter, who was caught trying to sell them for DM 180,000, a very sizeable amount. German authorities had been keeping the parties involved under surveillance for several months and finally made the snatch just minutes before the sale was consummated.

Lt. Col. Ryan was one of the first to be notified by the Munich Police; they advised him that the suitcase was being turned over to the Office of Restitution. Within minutes the Colonel called me and instructed me to "get over there right away for a first-hand look, and then talk to the head of the Criminal Division about getting a set of photographs of the key documents." One of our civilians, armed with a camera, accompanied me to the Police Commissioner's office in the *Rathaus* on Marienplatz. I had not been to that particular office before, but the building in which it was housed was among the most popular in the city; it contained the famous Glockenspiel.

After identifying ourselves, we were shown the suitcase and the documents. The most significant was the certificate signed by Hindenburg on 30 January 1933, appointing Hitler as Chancellor of the Reich. The remaining documents consisted of Hitler's Party Book No. 1, a weapons permit, passport, residence papers from Austria, World War I military papers plus several sketches he had made during that period, and a number of other items including a pocket watch engraved "A.H." The Criminal Police were very obliging when we asked if we could take pictures of the key documents. They had already taken photographs of the cache as soon as it was delivered to them, and had a set of prints ready for us to take back to the Colonel.

Later in the month, Lt. Col. Ryan advised he would like to meet at the House, with General Korseman, a former German general, to assess his opinions on a wide range of issues. These would cover the Korean War, the occupation of Germany, the attitudes of the German officers' corps toward the U.S. and Russia, plus questions on future rearmament of Germany. He suggested we record the conversation. This was easier said than done. We didn't have a tape recorder in our office, and neither did the main office. We discussed the requirement among ourselves at the House and made alternative plans.

On the day of the meeting, our two secretaries were in position with note pads in hand, behind the locked door closest to the Hitler-couch and table where Lt. Col. Ryan and General Korseman, plus another interested outsider, would be holding their discussion. I, as the interpreter, sat next to Lt. Col. Ryan. As far as I could tell, everything was running smoothly, and although I strained my ears, I couldn't detect a single sound coming from behind the door, not a sneeze or yawn, nor the squeak of a floorboard or a chair, nor the shuffling of feet; nothing, just absolute silence the way we planned it. When it was over more than an hour later and the General had gone, the girls let out a sigh of relief, their legs and arms cramped from sitting in the same position for such a prolonged time without moving a muscle except to take their shorthand notes. The verbatim transcript resulting from the awkward process was nevertheless superb.

The D.P. camp at Schleissheim was one of the places "our Russians" frequented, to pick up the latest tidbits on political activities within the displaced persons community and among Russian exile groups. I was fascinated at the reports they brought back on anti-communist activities deep within the Soviet Union. It was hard to believe that anti-government partisan groups were at work and able to exist within the confines of a dictatorial state that was well known for its ruthless methods of persecution and suppression of the people. When they reported having come upon a Russian military defector who had slipped into the camp, our main office wanted him picked up and brought in. There was no arrest. People like this defector were in West Germany of their own free will; they had cut their ties with the Soviet regime by defecting in the first place.

The fellow had been a lieutenant with the Soviet Army in East Germany. Our interrogator reported he spoke freely when he did the talking, but hedged under direct questioning and also when told to "just sit and write down everything" he knew. His was an unbelievable horror story. He told of tricking Germans (who had been betrayed by their neighbors because of their anti-communistic leanings) into coming to the *Kommandantur*, military government headquarters, where they were arrested and then executed. Their bodies were disposed of outside their hometown, in a section at the edge of a forest that had been roped off with signs posted: "Achtung—Minen," warnings of a live minefield.

I read the report before it was sent up the line; it was

upsetting. If this guy was telling the truth, I thought, then it must have happened in other places, too. How many more such occurrences had there been? Would we ever know? And if we knew, what could be done about it? The German within me started coming through again; I was boiling. I suddenly recalled reading as a child of the execution of thousands of Polish officers in the Katyn forest, near Smolensk, at the hands of the NKVD, the Russian Secret Police. That news had upset me to no end when I was fifteen, and eight years later there was still more of it, with an even more recent date. All I could say as I put the report on my desk was, "Those lousy good-for-nothing Russian bastards."

Lt. Col. Ryan was succeeded by Lt. Col. Smith during the summer of 1951. One of the first things on the schedule of the new S-2 was to visit one of the newly formed West German border protection units, the *Grenzschutz*, in their barracks near the Czech frontier. The Colonel wanted me to accompany him and function as interpreter, if needed. Arrangements had been made in advance with the Germans, and they welcomed the Colonel with proper military respect when we arrived at their kaserne. There were few formalities. After meeting with the German commander, he asked his deputy to take "the American inspector" on a tour of their facilities. I couldn't help but wonder if any of my former German schoolmates or Luftwaffenhelfer comrades might be back in uniform and serving with this outfit. It was doubtful that they'd be in West Germany, however; if anything, they'd be facing us from their dugouts beyond the tank ditches, operating under the protective umbrella of the Russians, their new masters.

We toured the German encampment rather quickly, paid our respects to the commander, and headed back to Munich. We were hardly on the road, when Lt. Col. Smith asked, "What was the size of that unit, Schroder?"

"That's kinda hard to say, sir. I know their C.O. was an Oberstleutnant, a lieutenant colonel, like you, and that the officer escorting us was a major, but other than that, I'd have to guess at it."

"Did you notice anything when we walked through the officers' mess?"

"No, except the tables were set for their next meal."

"Precisely. Did you notice how many place settings there were at the head table? That's where the C.O. and his field grade officers would be sitting. The company grade officers would be eating at the tables out in front."

"I never gave that a thought, Colonel; I'll have to remember that."

"Yes, they had a battalion there. It always pays to keep your eyes and ears open."

The short exchange with my boss proved once more that the learning process was never-ending, and that I had a long way to go before becoming expert in our business.

The work of our section was fascinating. There was never a dull moment, and always something different and challenging to do. I really enjoyed being a soldier. And, after getting the Good Conduct Medal, I wanted to stay in for another hitch, but I wanted to be sure I'd be able to continue serving in Germany, where I knew I could do a bang-up job. I waltzed into the Personnel Office at McGraw Kaserne sometime in mid-October, still a good four months from my discharge date, to "re-up" for three more years.

The clerk pulled my file, looked at me, and came back to the counter where I was standing. "Sorry, Schroder, but your name went to Washington two weeks ago. You'll be rotating in time to be home for Christmas."

"Oh, no, you can't mean it. Are you sure?"

"If you had come in two weeks earlier, we could have processed the paperwork so you could re-up, but once your name is in to Washington, it's too late, you can't change it. Sorry, buddy."

I wanted so much to stay, but I was caught up in the tide, just being pushed along without a rudder.

During the latter part of November, I received my orders to report to Bremerhaven by 9 December for reassignment to Camp Kilmer, New Jersey. From that time on, my remaining time in Munich just whittled away at lightning speed. There were a few get-togethers with friends and buddies, farewell parties, a last-minute promotion and even the presentation of a commendation from the commanding general. The send-offs completed, a delegation of friends from the House accompanied me to the Munich

Bahnhof and the train that would take me and a handful of other GIs from my unit to Bremerhaven, and then "home to America."

After almost fifteen years in Germany, I was on my way back to America, this time to rejoin my mother and sister, and start a new life, ready to face new challenges and grasp new opportunities. What more could I have asked for? I was one of the lucky ones: I'd come out of the cauldron of war and hate complete, with all my faculties intact, able to work for the tomorrow that not too long ago we could only dream of.

But parting was hard. I had been separated from house and home for a long time and often under very trying circumstances, so I had learned the ways of survival. I had experienced the misfortune of being on the losing side of world conflict; I had given up or lost many dear friends; and now I would be leaving behind forever the years of my youth, the places I cherished so dearly, where I grew up in hard times and under adverse conditions, and where I changed from a child to a youth to a man. I took what I could back to America, but part of me and my life would always remain in Germany. The train rolled through the night, and I cried.

Epilogue

The idea of getting home for Christmas triggered a round of celebrations among the troops aboard the naval ship *General H. F. Hodges*. We were especially excited at the sight of land, after riding out several days of rough seas. Men all around me rushed to the railings when the news of the sighting first broke, lining up three and four deep for a ringside look at that special place in the distance, their own America. For some, it had been years since they'd laid eyes on the magnificent view of the gateway to their great nation. And when we could make out the skyline of New York City, the skyscrapers and the Statue of Liberty, the laughter, cheers, whistling, and shouts of the men evidenced their happiness and joy.

These were exciting and fascinating moments for me as well. I had finally made it back to America. But after fifteen years I had become a stranger. I felt like an immigrant, not knowing what would come next. From the train that took us to Camp Kilmer I saw a forest of TV antennas atop high red brick buildings, garages and shacks. Most of the structures looked run down, drab and in need of repair; they all needed a good sprucing up, to say the least. I was disappointed. The sights before me were much less than what I had expected. There were evidently two sides to America, the facade of beauty as we perceived it from the sea, and then the realities of life in the "melting pot" of humanity. I figured from here on, life could be just as difficult in America as it had been for the people in postwar Europe, and I braced myself for the unknowns and uncertainties that would pop up when least expected.

The Army did a tremendous job. We arrived at Camp Kilmer on 23 December 1951, and they had us on our way to New York City the next day, in taxis and busses, to spend the Christmas holiday. This was when I realized I really wasn't alone in strange territory. I headed straight for Manhattan, where Aunt Edith and her family had settled down after being readmitted to the States. What a happy Christmas reunion it was. The timing was right, perfect for the start of a new life. And when I met my grandfather that afternoon, I hugged him hard and cried. I was overjoyed to see him again, and the tears flowed freely. Our thoughts were with my father, his son, still missing in action.

Right after the Christmas holiday I received leave orders allowing me to spend four whole weeks with my mother and sister in Rhode Island. We met and embraced amidst hugs and tears; we were together again. Mother had found work at a hospital in Providence, and my sister had become just another one of the kids at the local school.

After my discharge from the Army in early 1952, we moved to Pawtucket, where I had been born, and made it our home. I couldn't help but laugh; it seemed life had been playing games, and now the card said to return to "Go" and start all over.

Since I qualified as a Korean vet, the Veterans Administration representative came up with a clerical job for me at a nearby steel mill. My typing was primitive—strictly hunt and peck—but nevertheless fast and accurate, and the job was mine. I was delighted. I had overcome my greatest fear—that of not finding work. This indeed was my new beginning; I was now in the labor pool, off and running. A year or so later, I latched on to a trainee position in a wholesale building materials company, supported by the VA, which provided me with qualifications that came in handy later.

My interests had always been, and still were, in subjects of a military nature. That was how I had been brought up; that was all I really knew. The thought of going to college to acquire new skills while working to pay the tuition scared me. Knowing that thousands, even millions had done so right after the war was still not enough to convince me I could manage. I joined the Army Reserves instead, thinking I might go back on active duty one day. Besides, I kept telling myself, I owed the United States, and in particular the military, a debt. I wanted to repay them with my hard work for all they had done for me and my family. And, too, life in the private sector was boring to me; I missed the challenges of my days in Germany.

I decided to try my hand at taking the Federal Civil Service test. Perhaps this would open doors and provide alternative career opportunities. When I passed, however, I didn't get called; I kept trying. Finally, in 1960, I was hired as a procurement agent by Headquarters, Eighth Air Force, then based at Chicopee Falls, Massachusetts. It was hard for me to believe I would be working for the same air armada that had bombed the daylights out of Germany during the war while I watched them from the ground, scared and cussing. But these were the realities of life. I received my basic training and indoctrination into the labyrinth of government procurement at Westover Field, and was launched on a thirty-year civilian career with the U.S. Defense Department.

My life revolved around a small circle of friends, simply because there were few people with whom I had much in common. Most of the folks I encountered had all lived and labored in America during the war, and had learned to hate, or at least dislike, anything German. These were days when I listened a lot and said little.

In 1972, I took my wife Lora to Germany, my first trip back in twenty years, to show her where I had been stationed, first as a German soldier and then as a GI. Though it was a "Grand tour," we saw only half of what I would have liked to show her. The other half lay behind the barbed wire fences and minefields that separated West Germany from the East Zone, behind the notorious Iron Curtain. Near Bad Sooden-Allendorf, not too far from where Mother and Sister had made their daring escape years before, I stood at the border markers peering into the distance, wondering how my old school friends were making out, and too, whether my father had ever returned from the war to find our home abandoned. I walked away heavyhearted.

All these years, images of my father remained very vivid in my mind; his fate had been inconclusive, an open question to which I was forever seeking answers. So intense were my thoughts, that I dreamt of him several times each year. I saw him coming toward me in his grey uniform, wearing the riding breeches and the boots with spurs that he had worn the last time I had seen him in 1944. Our encounters were always in an area of sand dunes and shrubbery, with water in the distance. I had read of the final days of the war in East Prussia where Father had been stationed, and therefore knew the Soviets had driven the Germans toward or into the sea in the spring of 1945. Our dream meetings always ended with me desperately pleading for him to come home with me, telling him mother and sister were waiting. But he always replied that he couldn't, that his comrades needed him and that he had to get back in a hurry. At that, he turned about, heading away across the dunes and disappearing in the distance. I would wake up sobbing and in a sweat. The traumatic encounters weakened me physically and it usually took hours before I felt myself again.

Then, in May 1981, thirty-six years after the end of the war, I received a letter from the Red Cross advising that my father had been seen as a prisoner of the Soviets in Koenigsberg, East Prussia in early 1945. Many had died during the first winter of captivity, and my father was now thought to be among them. This letter contained the official and final word on the fate of my father. The dreams stopped.

My civilian career in the Defense Department included service in the field of procurement and contracting with the Air Force, Army, Defense Logistics Agency and, for the final twenty-one years, with the Navy. The career I pursued brought many challenges and many unexpected and difficult situations. To allow me to master my assignments, I finally came around and pursued a college degree, the American way. And, with the help of an excellent staff of dedicated and knowledgeable men and women, my office soon became known as the "tour de force" in our assigned area of contracting. Rear Admiral Benjamin F. Montoya, Commander of the Naval Facilities Engineering Command, and Chief of Civil Engineers, used this expression in presenting to me the Navy Superior Civilian Service Medal when I retired in 1989. I knew then that I had paid off my debts as I had intended, and I felt proud and thankful.

And when, just months later, the Berlin Wall gave way to the pressures of the German people, I realized how lucky and privileged our family had been to experience for over forty years the freedoms these people, our blood brothers and sisters, were just now beginning to enjoy.

Selected Further
Readings

Books

Beise, Karl-Walter. *Heil Hitler, Herr Lehrer*. Hamburg: Rohwohlt Verlag, 1983.

Bendiner, Elmer. *The Fall of Fortresses*. New York: G. P. Putnam's Sons, 1980.

Boberach, Heinz. *Jugend unter Hitler*. Duesseldorf: Droste Verlag, 1982.

Brown, William B. *Storming Hitler's Rhein: The Allied Assault, February–March 1945*. New York: St. Martin's Press, 1985.

Debecker, Gilbert. *Het Duitse Krijgsgevangenenkamp nummer 2228 van Overijse-Terlanen, Deel 2*. Leuven, Belgium: ACCO Druk, 1986.

Deighton, Len. *Blitzkrieg*. New York: Alfred A. Knopf, 1980.

Dulles, Allen. *The Secret Surrender*. New York: Harper & Row, 1966.

Eisenhower, Dwight D. *Crusade in Europe*. Garden City, N.Y.: Doubleday & Co., 1948.

Ellis, L. F., Major. *History of the Second World War; Victory in the West; Volume II, The Defeat of Germany*. London: HMSO, 1968.

Engelmann, Berndt. *In Hitler's Germany*. New York: Random House, 1986.

Goralski, Robert. *World War II Almanac 1931–1945*. New York: G. P. Putnam's Sons, 1981.

Haupt, Werner. *Als die Rote Armee nach Deutschland kam*. Friedberg, Germany: Podzun-Pallas Verlag, 1970.

Irving, David. *The Destruction of Dresden*. Northhamptonshire, U.K.: William Kimber & Co., 1963.

Lucas, James. *Last Days of the Third Reich*. New York: William Morrow & Co., 1986.

———. *World War Two through German Eyes*. London: Arms and Armour Press, 1987.

Muenchner Merkur. *Persoenlicher Nachlass Hitlers beschlagnahmt*. Munich: Muenchner Merkur, 16 December 1950.

Mondadori, Arnoldo. *2194 Days of War: An Illustrated Chronology of the Second World War*. New York: W. H. Smith Publishers, Gallery Books, 1988.

Nicolaisen, Hans-Dietrich. *Die Flak-Helfer*. Berlin: Verlag Ullstein, 1981.

Peterson, Edward N. *The American Occupation of Germany: Retreat to Victory*. Detroit: Wayne State University Press, 1977.

Richardson, Horst Fuchs, ed. *Sieg Heil! War Letters of Tank Gunner Karl Fuchs, 1937–1941*. Hamden, Conn.: Shoe String Press, Archon Books, 1987.

Ruhl, Klaus-Joerg. *Die Besatzer und die Deutschen*. Duesseldorf: Droste Verlag, 1980.

Scotland, A. P., Lt. Col., O. B. E. *The London District Cage*. London: Evans Brothers, 1957.

Speer, Albert. *Inside the Third Reich*. New York: Macmillan Co., 1970.

Stadtarchiv Minden. *Der totale Krieg und seine Folgen: Minden 1944 bis 1946*. Minden, Germany, Stadtarchiv Minden, 1975.

Toland, John. *Adolf Hitler*. New York: Ballantine Books, 1977.

War Department. *German 88-MM Antiaircraft Gun Materiel: War Department Training Manual No. E9-369A*. Washington, 29 June 1943. (Reprint)

Wistrich, Robert. *Who's Who in Nazi Germany*. New York: Outlet Book Co., Bonanza Books, 1982.

Military Histories

The Army Air Forces in World War II: Combat Chronology, 1941–1945. Office of Air Force History, Headquarters USAF, 1973.

Combat History of 354th Infantry Regiment. Colorado Springs, Colo.: H & H Printing, 1985.

The 89th Infantry Division 1942–1945. History of 89th Infantry Division. n.d.

We Ripened Fast. Unofficial History of the 76th Infantry Division, 76th Division Officers' Association, Baltimore, Md.

Letters and Interviews

Banbery, J. C. England, 1988. British paratrooper of 'B' Squadron, 6th Airborne Armoured Recce Regiment. Served as wireless operator and loader in the lead Cromwell tank dubbed "Swan-on-II"; on 4 April

1945, fired at German 88s emplaced near town of Holzhausen II on road to Minden.

Buckley, Tom. England, 1988. British paratrooper of 'C' Squadron, 6th Airborne Armoured Recce Regiment, the unit that was shot up by German flak on 4 April 1944. Was on Bren gun carrier that was able to avoid the German gunfire. Returned with reinforcements.

Institut fuer Zeitgeschichte. Munich, 11 November 1977. Provided data on Generals Wolff, Felmy and Gareis.

James, Gerry. A member of the British 4.2″ mortar troop of the 6th Airborne Armoured Recce Regiment. Taken prisoner during the 4 April 1945 firefight near Holzhausen II; liberated by U.S. forces on 10 April.

Kamp 2228 Komitee. Overijse, Belgium, 3 August 1989. Provided copy of layout of Camp 2228 and photos of camp.

Kendall, H. O. England, 1987. British paratrooper of 22d Independent Company, 6th Airborne Division: the unit that stormed German flak position on 4 April 1945.

Leithold, Eberhard. German Luftwaffenhelfer who escorted British POWs to the town of Stemmer on 4 April 1945. On returning, saw his unit being taken prisoner. Made his way eastward with other retreating Germans, reaching Werdau, his hometown, two days after the Americans took city.

Nussmann, Werner. Germany, January 1990, former POW, Camp 2228, LaHulpe, Belgium.

Siegel, Erich. Germany, November 1989, former POW, Camp 2228, LaHulpe, Belgium.